My ~~My~~ OUR President Has Balls!

OUR My President™
HAS BALLS!

An Examination of the
Cultural Divide in America Today

FRANK MASCETTI

MILTON RAE
PRESS

My (Our) President Has Balls!

An Examination of the Cultural Divide in America Today

Published in New York, New York, by Milton Rae Press, an imprint of Morgan James Publishing. Morgan James is a trademark of Morgan James, LLC. www.MorganJamesPublishing.com

ISBN 9781642794342 paperback
ISBN 9781642794359 eBook
Library of Congress Control Number: 2019930799

Cover Design by:
Megan Dillon
megan@creativeninjadesigns.com

Interior Design by:
Chris Treccani
www.3dogcreative.net

MILTON RAE
P R E S S
A BRANDED IMPRINT
OF MORGAN JAMES

For my two wonderful children, Brittany (twenty) and Christopher (sixteen). For it is their generation and the generations beyond that inspired me to write this book.

ACKNOWLEDGMENTS

Any project, whether personal or in business, requires a team of people to accomplish. Without my particular team, this project would not have been possible. I would like to acknowledge them here:

- **Americans:** I want to thank inventors, heroes, politicians (current and past), members of the FBI, the "silent majority," our forefathers, and the broad group of Americans who assisted me indirectly.
- **Google:** Various research and statistics stated in this book came from Google searches. I saved an immense amount of time by collaborating data.
- **The media:** Referenced on many occasions, various news outlets contributed to my understanding of our current culture and political landscape.
- **My kids:** Brittany and Christopher; it is because of their future I was so passionate about this project.

- **Interviewees:** Although their names have been changed to protect their identities, they provided some great insight and perspective.
- **Friends at "The Duck" Tavern:** Friends at the local pub provided inspiration and contributed several topics and content.
- **My English Teacher, Essex Community College:** Around 1975 or 1976, a teacher once wrote on one of my papers, "Please write for money." My name wasn't on this piece of work; however, she knew it was mine from earlier writings. We had a discussion, and she said the paper had the quality to be posted in *The New York Times* editorial section. She knew I was pursuing a career as an electrical engineer but still encouraged me to write. It's taken me just forty-two short years, but I am following that advice. Better later than never, I guess!
- **Gerry Czarnecki:** A neighbor and writer, he helped me navigate the process of editing and publishing this work.
- **David Hancock:** Founder of Morgan James Publishing, allowed me this opportunity to publish this work and provided great insight along the way.
- **The Editorial Attic:** Angie Kiesling and her team were masters at providing editing insight and getting this author to rethink certain portions of the book.

Finally, I would like to personally thank **Lee Arrowood.** A longtime business associate of twenty-plus years, Lee wrote seven books. After reading his *Delusional: Death of a Startup*, I became inspired to finally write a first book of my own.

I'm certain I have missed others who have helped me along the way of this long journey. For my son, Chris, who often asked, "You're working on your book . . . again?" As quite a bit of the writing was completed on weekends when he was staying with me, I appreciate that he was sensitive to this project and very supportive.

CONTENTS

PREFACE

Upon first glance, I imagine you, the reader, would immediately believe this book is about the current president of the United States, Donald J. Trump, and that the writer has a strong opinion or bias. In fact, this book is really about two things: one, cultural changes and division in America over the last forty to fifty years; and two, the current crisis of our democracy. The fact of the matter is that our current president has brought a lot of attention to various issues plaguing America and its people today. Like him or not, he is tackling crucial issues: the economy, regulations, immigration, healthcare, foreign relations, the drug epidemic, terrorist threat, and other concerns that impact the lives of every citizen. This president has not chosen the path of least resistance but the road that has been less traveled by presidents in the recent past.

While I realize a large portion of this book is about President Trump, I encourage the reader to have an open mind. I'm truly hoping we might agree on one thing: "American culture has changed for the worst, and this situation didn't happen overnight—and certainly didn't happen over the last eighteen months or even nine years." As an example, let's take the week of September 11, 2018.

Comedian Bill Maher knocked excessive patriotic bulls**t and militarism at US sporting events. This was the same week that people were remembering the loss of loved ones that occurred on September 11, 2001. This is the same clown—uh, comic—who said the following, one week after the infamous 9/11 terror attacks: "We have been the cowards, lobbing cruise missiles from two thousand miles away. That's cowardly. Staying in the airplane when it hits the building, say what you want about it, it's not cowardly." Advertisers started pulling out, and his show, *Political Incorrectness*, was pulled from the air. I absolutely understand our First Amendment rights to free speech, but do the people who make such comments realize that if they said such things about countries in other parts of the world, their body would be cut up into pieces and spread around that country?

In November 2016, one of the largest upsets in American presidential elections was realized. Like most everyone else, I have an opinion as to what might have transpired that Tuesday, November 8. While many people might not have put the "Trump" signs on their lawns, the bumper stickers on the cars, or even told their husbands, wives, boyfriends, girlfriends, and friends who they were voting for, they went into that voting booth and did what most people do: *they voted against the candidate they dislike more.* This explanation alone represents the decision of a very good percentage of the voting population.

While I am a Republican National Committee supporter and was originally committed to voting for Marco Rubio, he lost my vote in the latter stages of the debates when he was trying to play "Trump's game." You see, another large part of the population was simply frustrated with Washington DC, the constant gridlock on important issues facing our nation, and the political correctness that seems to have overtaken our democracy. In addition, many in business had seen hundreds of thousands of manufacturing jobs moved offshore, with such parent companies as Cisco, Agilent, Burger King, Budweiser, Purina, Seagate, Frigidaire, and even Good Humor. The Chinese had taken our intellectual property, and we were then letting them take the parent companies as well. What the h***? A good many Americans were looking for a successful businessman to save this train wreck of a nation and steer us through these tumultuous times. After all, the United States had nearly twenty trillion dollars in debt at the time.

So, I ask this simple question of every person reading this book, no matter your political affiliation: how many times have you witnessed past elections and said, "I wish the candidates would stop telling us what we wanted to hear and just tell it like it is"? Well, for those of us who read business books in the 80s, 90s, and early 2000s, including Lee Iacocca's *Talking Straight*, Jack Welch's *Straight from the Gut*, Thomas Peters's *In Search of Excellence*, and the famous Donald Trump's *Art of the Deal*, we already knew Donald Trump was an outspoken egotist who liked winning, bragging about his success, and belittling the loser. He would tell it like it is.

As I begin writing this book on April 9, 2018, the United States is faced with a nuclearized North Korea, Syria's chemical weapons usage, and growing threats in Iran, Russia, and

China. I certainly don't know how each of these situations will play out—I am no different than you—but I do know this: ~~My~~ (Our) President Has Balls!™ He sees the world as it really is, not as how it should be. After all, past presidents have faced the same bad actors; maybe we now need to try a different approach. In US history books to date, George Washington, Andrew Jackson, Teddy Roosevelt, and Ronald Reagan certainly would rate as "bad a****."

Unfortunately, we live in a world of corrupt regimes, dictatorships, jihadists, and others who would like to annihilate the United States, its people, and most of Western civilization. They simply cannot relate to our convictions and what we stand for; it's no different than the way we view their hardcore convictions. Many of us cannot relate to the thousands of men and women serving our country day in and day out, sleeping with one eye open, thousands of miles from their family and friends. Most of us wouldn't want to be there but are proud that our men and women in service are. To back them up, I like to know that ~~my~~ (our) president has balls and makes these bad actors nervous, not knowing what his next move might be.

American culture as we know it is also coming under siege from some of our own people. My intention in the writing of this book is to help us all open our minds a little bit, reflect on our past, and look forward to how we might all contribute to a better future. It's not about one man or one woman. This is *our* America, and we all share the responsibility of what America is. Our enemies are watching both from afar and within, and they want us at odds with one another. This makes us weaker as a country and precisely what the Russians and Chinese, as examples, would want.

And what of social media and various news media sources? What's very surprising to me is that we have to be our own reporters today to verify facts from various news sources. It seems we can't trust certain sources, books, or social media outlets for information. We've never before had to have such a critical eye. When I was a kid, all we had to do was go down to the basement and grab the encyclopedia. We believed everything we read. Being an engineer myself and very analytical, I rely on data, typically from several sources, to confirm a procedure or opinion. I just don't see this investigative process happening today. Everyone in politics seems to be offering opinion or perspective *rather than facts*, and that's simply dangerous.

I wanted to share a letter that I wrote on December 12, 2016, just one month after the presidential election. I didn't send the letter to anyone or post it on Facebook. The purpose of the letter was to vent a little and express my feelings as to what was going on at the time. Like many Americans, I was rather confused, so I expressed my feelings here. The title is "I Am an American . . . Are You?"

Please don't attempt to read between the lines to determine whether I am a Democrat, Republican, or independent. *I am 100 percent American* and have become increasingly concerned over the views of other Americans. I cannot understand how we are not sharing the same values, set on some very fundamental things. What happened? After the ugliest of all political contests I have ever witnessed in my lifetime, I have some questions for my fellow Americans:

Why would any American want to see our own people starving on the streets, hooked on heroin in inner-city neighborhoods, struggling inner-city neighborhoods, yet want to allow for illegal immigration to our country . . . no matter where these illegals come from? Are entitlement programs a way to simply get the problem off a bureaucrat's desk, moving on to something he feels is more important?

My family (and most likely yours) emigrated to America through a legal process, many coming from Italy and Ireland at that time. These people from other lands brought their own hardships and unique challenges; however, they came through a legal process. In addition, they wanted to be Americans and were proud of our flag and what we stood for. Wouldn't my fellow Americans want immigrants today to enter the same way, "paying in" to our society so that other Americans aren't footing the bill for their medical and other expenses while legal citizens are dying on our streets? Aren't we all in 100 percent agreement here? It seems we would rather talk about a wall, a grand wall, a this and that . . . rather than the root cause of such a discussion. Are we all this naïve?

With so many government employees managing various programs, why aren't we mad about the wasteful spending? I have firsthand knowledge of a skilled nursing facility costing over seven thousand dollars per person, two women sharing a single room. At fourteen thousand dollars per month, these helpless people are confined to a bed and require very little care. The government foots the bill once people go broke (and you will). Where does all this money go that the government is wasting on such programs? Why are these costs so ridiculously high? Aren't we all mad over this?

Regarding our healthcare system, aren't we continuing to discuss the wrong things? Obamacare, this care, that care? What does it matter? Isn't the real problem at the root of it all? How can an operation cost thousands of dollars less at one facility versus another? A short weekend hospital stay of three nights runs up a tab of over seventy thousand dollars, and the insurance companies are paying? That's the real problem in the first place, isn't it? Aren't we all angry over this? These two items alone are costing all American taxpayers.

Entitlement programs for inner-city Americans have created generations of people on welfare programs and food stamps. Doesn't this get all Americans mad? I get the impression that many Americans feel we aren't doing enough here, yet what are we really doing to help these people be more involved, more a part of society, and to fit in? They do not. They feel their country has let them down, and it's an us-against-them mentality.

World War III . . . we have said for many years before that this war was coming and would be with the Middle East. Don't all Americans want to be safe in our homes, on our streets, and globally free to travel whenever and wherever we might want to? Why are we compelled to show and discuss every single aspect of our military on major news networks and then have various critics come on and attack and analyze? Who do you think is watching all this stuff? We never had internet or cable TV when General Patton and other greats were planning their military strategies. As Americans, we simply trusted that those in charge would make the right decisions and kill those trying to kill us first. Don't we all agree on this point?

After traveling to many parts of the world and seeing the other side, I can say I am a proud American and happy to be living in this country. I certainly haven't always agreed with presidential choices in my life; however, once the election results are in, I stand by and support my new commander in chief. Why? Because the process has spoken, and it's time to move on. Again, please don't try and attack my words, read between the lines, or think that I have some hidden agenda here. My sole purpose in writing this brief is to wonder whether or not all Americans share the same core values.

Thanks for picking up a copy of this book, and I hope you enjoy reading it as much as I truly enjoyed writing it.

CHAPTER 1

Short-Term Memory

On the morning of September 11, 2001, America was forever changed. For those old enough to remember, we can recall precisely where we were that day and the emotions we felt then and for the days, weeks, and months that followed. After the events unfolded that horrible Monday morning in 2001, we found out that the pilots flying the planes that crashed into the World Trade Center and Pentagon were actually trained right here in our own backyard, in Opa Locka, Florida.

But, we all stood together, shoulder to shoulder, as unified Americans, with no party differences or in-your-face politics.

Many of us bought American flags and proudly displayed these on our cars, in our homes, and in our hearts. We were somber together. We were upset together. We cried together. We despised an enemy combatant together. We were one people together. Just seventeen years later, what has happened to these same compassionate, united Americans? Could America have really changed this much? Do we all see how much we have changed as a people and a country?

Just six years after 9/11, in December 2007, our country suffered the worst economic downturn since the Great Depression that started in 1929. The subprime mortgage crisis and lending practices were the major contributors to this catastrophe that lasted nineteen months, to June 2009. President Barack Obama navigated us through this horrific period of time. During this crisis, the worst financial crisis of my lifetime, I recall friends curbing spending habits and no longer contributing to their 401ks. Even the market giant Starbucks had to make changes to its product line and growth plan.

It wasn't such a very long time ago now, but it seems many Americans have a very short-term memory for such things. As a matter of point, I'll bet that if you ask ten people about Starbucks decision to eliminate decaffeinated coffee during that time, they will not recall the situation. The point is, the Seattle company was forced to shut three hundred of their stores and lay off six thousand people. Their net income fell 69 percent alone that quarter. You can reference a *New York Times* article by Claire Cain Miller, January 29, 2009, if you want to google it and fact-check me.

Due to the catastrophic events surrounding the Great Recession, companies performed knee-jerk reactions in an attempt to control costs and debt. Dunkin' Donuts stopped selling all frozen drinks; convenience stores stopped displaying all types of products at their checkout areas. Many people were taking out large sums of cash to store in their homes. The point is, the crisis happened so quickly, we didn't know what tomorrow would bring.

And what about ISIS? After we toppled Saddam Hussein in 2003, the original al-Qaeda group gained more power and strength. Every day, the United States was threatened by this group of jihadist terrorists who wanted to destroy our Western culture and civilization. Donald Trump vowed to "wipe them out" if he became president, and he has all but done that. We talk very little about ISIS today or what has actually been accomplished in this area. Remember the threats? Remember being afraid to travel overseas or even attend outdoor cultural events? It's incredible to me that I now see posts on Facebook every day as friends travel the world again.

For a nation that seemed so united in 2001, how is it we have become so divided? We should all know the age-old adage, safety in numbers. Our enemies do, and they are united and well organized. As a nation and a country, we are not. Having a difference of opinion is one thing, but spewing hatred against the other party and not doing what's right for your country and its citizens just doesn't seem right. While you read this book, I simply ask that you have an open mind as to what might seem like one person's opinion or personal rant. (I tend to have those but will try to control myself for the sake of the reader.)

Whether we like it or not, we live in the richest and most powerful country in the world, with the strongest economy and strongest military. While we don't often consider these particular strengths, each of us enjoys the direct benefits of our position as American citizens every day. Whether it's scrolling on Facebook, going to the movies, enjoying a sporting event, or any of the other hundreds of comforts we simply take for granted every day, we must remember millions upon millions of people around the world are less fortunate. For those of us who have been fortunate to travel and have visited less-civilized countries, how many of us have said, "I cannot wait to get back home"? We may miss the electricity, infrastructure, plumbing, restaurants in America, or so many other things that we normally enjoy without much thought. Let's not forget the many brave men and women who have fought to allow these rights and privileges we enjoy or forget the important aspects of our history that separate us from other nations.

We are a rich and diverse culture of people. Through business travel, I have come to know colleagues from Meridian, Mississippi, to Boston, Massachusetts, to Flowery Branch, Georgia, to Santa Barbara, California. All are so diverse. I love my country because of its people. Let's try to open our minds if, in fact, they are closed. Let's stop spewing hatred toward one another and get back to being the Americans we were before September 11, 2001. While it's impossible to control how another person might behave or communicate, we must remember positivity starts with us and is contagious.

While some have short-term memory regarding the patriotism and unity we enjoyed pre-9/11, I truly hope that our current divisiveness and downright hatred of one another shall soon become a very distant memory, too. Perhaps because one can hide behind tweets, text messages, and emails, hostile but not directly confrontational communication is allowed daily. This should not be.

Growing up in Baltimore, I have fond memories of Fourth of July celebrations. I would walk home through the various alleys and see who was having a cookout in their backyard. You didn't need to know the family as the backyard was open to anyone who cared to enter. You went in, enjoyed a hotdog or burger and a soda, and relaxed in each other's company, sharing the day's events, talking about family and where you lived.

So long as I remember, Democrats and Republicans were a part of our country's story; however, I don't recall such a political divide between the members of each party in my younger years. We sat out on our porches, talked to our neighbors, and were truly one people. We all shared a common sense of good, although our lives and ambitions might have been vastly different.

I suppose I'm quite passionate about what has become of our great country and its people today. Our younger generation likely think the New England Patriots were always a dynasty in football, just as they will believe politics has always been ugly. For those of us a little older (and perhaps wiser), we know differently. Vicious, extremely polarized language and a mind-set of not working together for the betterment of the country may be the norm today, but it hasn't always been so.

While the two parties, Democrat and Republican, have been divided as long as they've existed—over 226 years now—it's much harder to meet in the middle now than in days long gone. Have we gone so far to the right or the left that the middle is gone altogether? Have both parties become so comfortable in their attacks of each other that they'd rather continue these attacks than compromise? Hopefully, for the sake of our people and country, our memory of this divisive time in history will be short-lived, replaced with better times, more compromise, more listening, and less attacking. Because if we look at our recent history—the last ten years or so—it's a really ugly snapshot of who we are.

CHAPTER 2

The Trump Complex

F riends of mine, who know me all too well, this chapter is dedicated to you. For those of you who don't know me, you might get to know me "just a little" by the end of this chapter.

I was raised in a lower-middle-class neighborhood in the Dundalk suburb of southeast Baltimore, Maryland. My father, his brother, his dad, and so many others in this Dundalk neighborhood worked at the Sparrows Point steel mill, often referred to as "the Point." The Sparrows Point complex was part of Bethlehem Steel, and my dad was a crane operator in the tin mill there. Off to work in the wee hours before dawn and home by 2:45 p.m. every day, it was the family dinner at four thirty each night of my entire upbringing.

Six of us shared a three-bedroom, twelve-thousand-dollar row home in the Charlesmont neighborhood of Dundalk. My sister got her own bedroom, so that left the three brothers to share a bedroom. The home had only one bathroom, but I never recall anyone having an "incident." We had one bath, one TV, one used car—no PlayStation, smartphones, Facebook, Google, or any of the other crutches we have become accustomed to today. If you wanted to know something or do research, you either asked your parent or searched the encyclopedias in your basement. In the *Encyclopedia Brittanica*, you found the "real news," all the answers you needed to guide you through life as we knew it.

Don't get me wrong. As an electrical engineer, I'm all for technology. Progress is a natural occurrence, and in a later chapter, I will speak to how some of these technologies have impacted our lives today, but my childhood was a simpler time, and I have fond memories of the slower pace of life.

I had very humble beginnings and am now a long way from where my journey began, for sure. But, nonetheless, being raised in the Dundalk suburb of Baltimore, in the Mid-Atlantic region of the country, had countless benefits. Simply put, people there "tell it like it is." (Just ask my sister!) My Italian grandparents, Ettore and Mary, as well as my Italian Aunt Rita, Uncle Art, Uncle Johnny, always told it like it was. There was no sugarcoating words on that side of my family. I didn't know any different behavior or way of seeing the world than what was demonstrated by the people I grew up around. Their responses were not rehearsed; rather, their words were fresh and had meaning. Maybe this is why there were so many fights when I was younger; things happened spontaneously. Regardless of the fights, this unrehearsed, authentic way of being together is how we made best friends that lasted a lifetime.

Although my dad earned a modest income in those days (the 60s), he sent all of his children to a private Catholic school, we ate steak at least once a week (fish on Fridays), and he took us out to dinner once a week. Two of our favorite dinner spots were The White Swan in Millers Island and Ho Joy Chinese restaurant in Essex. Go figure, The White Swan had some of the freshest seafood around and Maryland was famous for that, but I *always* ordered the famous Maryland fried chicken . . . not the rockfish they were known for.

You know the saying, "You don't know what you don't know." Now having traveled for both business and pleasure—to Scotland, England, Germany, Italy, Paris, South of France (notice I broke that out!), Hawaii five times, Bermuda, and all throughout the Caribbean and the United States—I have truly come to appreciate my roots more than ever. My great affection for the people back in that Dundalk area has only grown. In the Mid-Atlantic region, you will meet some of the warmest, nicest, and best-looking people our country has to offer.

We will now fast-forward as I make my point. I graduated from the University of Maryland, College Park, in 1980 with a bachelor's of science in electrical engineering. Having watched my dad, uncle, Popi, and so many friends work at "the Point," I knew I didn't want to work there. I wanted to be an electrical engineer at Westinghouse by the Baltimore airport, and this is the job I eventually landed right out of college. I had a wonderful girlfriend at the time who was completely supportive of my education, as were her parents. However, after interviewing with a company in Miami that was offering a 30 percent pay increase over what I was making at Westinghouse, I left my family, my girlfriend, and all my friends to move to Hollywood, Florida.

I had a friend who had moved to Hollywood a couple years earlier, so I shacked up with "Animal" for a few crazy months. The rent was cheap, and I recall paying to have the gas turned on so I could at least heat a pot of water for tea. When I moved there in March of 1981, Animal was a bartender at the world-famous Diplomat Hotel. Needless to say, his hours were very late, partying to the wee hours of the morning, and he was usually still up when I was getting up for work in the mornings. Animal had gone to school at Cardinal Gibbons in Baltimore and was one of the smartest guys I knew at that time. (Although my dad had a ninth grade education, he had fought in the Korean War and was actually the smartest guy I knew.)

Telling it like it is or, as I often refer to it today, the "Trump Complex," was very natural for Animal as well. I recall the night we got in a gang fight in the parking lot of the Agora Ballroom nightclub because Animal was harassing some guys inside the club. As Animal and I were surrounded by five tall black men in the parking lot of the nightclub, I recall one of the guys asking Animal, "So, what you got on your chest?" Animal was rather burly and said, "I got beef on my chest."

Knowing it was a matter of seconds before a fight ensued and trusting my instincts, I threw the first punch. Luckily, the police came quickly and broke it up. For the three short months I lived with Animal before I could find a place of my own, I recall taking a trip to the Florida Keys for the weekend. Animal was left back at the duplex where we lived on Dewey Street in Hollywood. The back door to our place had been kicked in that weekend by a jealous husband, so Animal cut up some old tennis shoes to make hinges to put the door back in place. I'll save that story for another book.

Given all the drama, I decided to get an apartment and move closer to work in Miami. So, I moved to the Village Oaks apartment complex in Miami Lakes. Some of the best times of my life were at that complex as most of the people were young professionals from all over the country who had moved to Miami soon after college to start their own careers as well (flight attendants, pilots, associates at Burdines, and professionals from Racal-Milgo's corporate offices). Many Miami Dolphins' rookies were also residents of that apartment complex. The famous Don Shula was also a resident of Miami Lakes, with an American flag proudly displayed on his basketball backboard, as well as a few Fords parked in the driveway.

As we partied at the pool in our complex on the weekends and I got acquainted with all my new friends from New England, Indiana, Pittsburgh, Minnesota, and other parts of the country, everyone who came in contact with me soon knew me by the saying, "Excuse me for being myself." While it might take me two years to select new living room furniture, my communication skills have always been rather impulsive. Yes, this has gotten me into a little trouble over the years; however, this Trump Complex has actually reaped more rewards than penalties for me.

Being single until I was thirty-nine years old and living in South Florida for nearly twenty years before I was married, I had many dates and girlfriends. To this day, I simply don't understand one thing about women. Most women will say they want an honest man who will tell it like it is and not play games, but, boy, do I have stories about some of the truths I have told, including a first date on which the girl was brought to tears, claiming what a horrible man I was.

Simply put, can we handle the truth? Do we need to take a deep breath before speaking and weigh the possible outcome and repercussions of our comments? If we do that, will the conversation have the same outcome and purpose? Will it be *real*, or will it simply be what the other party wanted to hear? Do we need to politicize all of our conversations?

For me, based on my upbringing and the part of the country in which I was raised, I appreciate candor and fresh, impulsive dialogue. I can handle it, but I am not so sure about kids today. Society now frowns on such impulsiveness. I, however, will make no excuses for my Trump Complex, and at the vintage age of sixty years, I don't believe my conversation style will change anytime soon. I also don't make any excuses for our president as I know his impulsive tweets and comments are real, whether we like them or not.

However, I will make an excuse for the media coverage today and the "fake news" label that's been applied, implying this content is not so real. I believe three key factors are at play:

1. **Spin:** It's been this way since the beginning of time; the author predicts how the audience will receive his or her message and "spins" the story so it's a bit more exciting.
2. **Internet:** Simply put, today's newspaper is yesterday's news. More timely venues now break news stories, including Facebook, Google, Twitter, and other live feeds.
3. **Sensationalism:** When I grew up, we had three to six stations on TV, no cable news, and only local channels. Now, the major networks turn to sensationalism to make their stories more exciting so they can compete in a world where spin and internet dominate.

So, before you pass judgment on this president for his spontaneous tweets, just remember that his perspective is fresh, unrehearsed, and, in many cases, not even prepared. He's just being himself, and I doubt that at his age he will change this behavior anytime soon. Sometimes, we may not like the person, but we cannot deny his accomplishments. Certainly, a very long list of people fit in this category, but I will just throw out two quick examples inspired by my passion for the NFL.

First, let's consider Tom Brady. I am a die-hard Dolphins fan; hence, I am probably more critical of Brady's demeanor, smugness, and "baby" attitude than others may be. In fact, I'll admit I am hypercritical of the Patriots quarterback. I believe that Bill Belichick created Tom Brady. Even so, in the end, I cannot deny the player's accomplishments.

Next up is Cam Newton. According to my friends who live in the Carolinas, Cam is often hated, even by the fans. I like the guy and rooted for him in Super Bowl 50, yet the media and many haters had a reason to pick on the guy.

When it comes to supporting a US president, unlike our opinions on NFL teams, we must all stand together, shoulder to shoulder, behind that president for the term of his presidency . . . no matter what. You can dislike the person, but you should respect the position. We are not in his position; we will never realize the hundreds of stressful decisions he might make daily on our behalf. What we see might be a tweet, and then we'll hear countless days of spin around his particular words. I'll leave it for each reader to decide how you will deal with these situations or pass judgment.

It takes an awful lot of courage to say and do some of the things Trump has said and done to date. How many times did our parents tell us, as children, to speak up for ourselves and stand our ground? Did we? Or, did we take the easier way and avoid confrontation for fear of what might happen? Consequences for speaking up and standing our ground are sure to come. And when Donald Trump has confronted far-left issues, it has brought out the worst in some citizens. People are absolutely flipping out as they feel their liberties are being violated. This president says what many of us are thinking. He is a businessman who looks at the world and issues as black and white, very much like a balance sheet.

Back to football. Because of my dislike of the New England Patriots, I have my own theory on why they lost to the New York Giants twice and my own opinions on Deflate Gate and those infamous footballs. However, if you discuss such things with a Patriots fan, he'll offer a completely different perspective. Fair?

But we're not talking football or Super Bowls where two teams compete. We are talking about the United States of America, one president and one team. We're all on this same team and should all be rooting to win. Right?

There's a lot to be said regarding a person's upbringing and where she is from. I used to travel to Long Island quite frequently for business and got to know the people from that area well. I can assure you; they are not a shy, introverted people. They are aggressive and passionate. Donald Trump hails from this region, and it's rather amusing to me that his demeanor and manor would be so shocking to people. Really? Just because people can be outspoken or have aggressive behavior doesn't mean that they aren't compassionate, loving, or caring individuals. We are all different and should respect each other for who we are.

Former multibillionaires who seek public office certainly not running for a popularity contest because they've already won the esteem of the country. Take, for example, Jerry Jones, Al Davis, George Steinbrenner, Bill Gates, Wayne Huzienga, and, of course, Donald J. Trump. Take note of the egos as you evaluate these guys, many of whom owned professional sports teams paying players millions of dollars per year. This is a special league of characters with flamboyant, outspoken, and sometimes abrasive personalities. They got to the top through hard work and by the willingness to make tough decisions; in many instances, they succeeded because they had the confidence that comes from believing they could do no wrong. How many of us can identify with George Steinbrenner? Jerry Jones? Al Davis? Tough characters, for sure. I'd have to say that a few of these guys have "The Trump Complex" as well.

CHAPTER 3

No Political Baggage

Donald Trump is not beholden to any special interest groups or lobbyists and entered his presidency with no political baggage. While his constant refrain of "drain the swamp" might strike a chord with so many politicians, how many of these same politicians have been enriched by various special interest groups? The top interest group, as an example, is lawyers. They contributed *over fifty-five million dollars* so far in 2018 to various congressional personnel; 75 percent of those funds went to Democrats. If you closely evaluate this money trail, you will see millions upon millions of dollars of enrichments here.

Do you recall when Trump was first putting together his cabinet personnel? A specific requirement for potential members was zero involvement with special interest groups or lobbyists. From the onset, he let Americans know he would be his own person, representing the ideals of the American people who put him into office. It's hard not to respect that.

When he was running in the primary, with at least sixteen candidates running to be the Republican presidential candidate, one could hardly argue he was running for a popularity contest or was beholden to a particular special interest group or had anyone in his pocket. He spoke from the heart, was extremely candid, and said the things that were on many Americans' minds at the time.

While being an outsider certainly has its advantages, disadvantages also exist. For example, just as he is not beholden to any special interest groups or lobbyists, he is not beholden to any specific politician either. We've witnessed riffs with Paul Ryan, Marco Rubio, Mitch McConnell, Rand Paul, John McCain, and countless others. We should always have expected turnover in various positions in his cabinet, as turnover has been part of his businesses. While he can offer fresh insight to old topics and say things others in his party might only be thinking, this candor can have consequences.

The irony is that Trump is not a prior politician, nor is he political. Yet, half of the country, as well as liberal media outlets, want to politicize every action taken or word spoken. When he speaks at a rally or sends a tweet, he offers fresh perspective with little to no rehearsal. By comparison, how many people touch or review a news story before it is released or "spun" into its final version?

It's interesting to note that having no political baggage or prior political experience is probably the single point that gave Trump the most challenges in his first twenty months in office. He doesn't care what he says. He gets mad with those in his own party when key policies the American people wanted are not advanced.

President Trump, however, does need the support of his party—and some support from the other party—to accomplish his agenda. That being said, he must learn the political system and how to win some of these people over.

It's interesting to me to observe the behaviors of those who ran against Trump in the presidential primary, a very ugly race. They are now some of his strongest supporters (i.e., Marco Rubio, Rand Paul, and Lindsey Graham). Even Mitt Romney was up for a possible post within the administration after lambasting Trump in 2016 when he said, "If we Republicans choose Donald Trump as our nominee, the prospects for a safe and prosperous future are greatly diminished." Ironically, Mitt Romney is still a strong supporter of Donald Trump today, predicting he will win again in 2020.

Career politicians in this day and age seem to be beholden to the mighty dollar more than to the people they were elected to serve. They pour themselves into new books, speaking tours, or a shot at being a contributor on a major news network. They court special interest groups and organizations in areas that might enrich their lives financially. While these same politicians seem to bark loudly about drug epidemics taking over the country, our poor communities, climate change, and so many other topics, I wonder just how many actually visit the inner-city communities having such a difficult time? While they earn their millions and stuff their own coffers, flying private jets to their next destination, how many career politicians are simply all talk and no action? How many are tape recording private meetings and keeping special notebooks to use such information in a future bestseller?

I simply ask, what the h*** is going on here? Are we so gullible as to believe the lines we are fed by these swamp creatures? Both sides of the aisle, mind you. This situation is not a one-party problem. Our taxpayer dollars go directly toward the salaries of these knuckleheads, and it appears the American people showed just how frustrated they were with Washington, DC when they voted for Donald J. Trump. He certainly wasn't quiet on the campaign trail and was quite vocal as he attacked some very specific policies and issues facing our country today. It was also obvious that he wasn't bought and paid for like so many others who had to say certain things, do certain things, and support certain things to appease those who were financially supporting them.

Let's take an even closer look at what these swamp creatures pass into law and what they do in their actual lives today. I will let the reader decide if this appears to be self-serving. The children of Congress members do not have to pay back their college student loans. Staffers of Congress family members are also exempt from having to pay back student loans. Members of Congress can retire at full pay after serving only one term in office. Members of Congress have exempted themselves from many of the laws that they have passed, under which ordinary citizens must live. For example, they are exempt from any fear of prosecution for sexual harassment. The latest example is that they have exempted themselves from Healthcare Reform, in all of its aspects. Why is it that we tolerate such an elite class of people, elected as public servants and then putting themselves above the very laws that they pass? A proposed 28ᵗʰ Amendment to the United States Constitution suggests "Congress shall make no law that applies to the citizens of the United States that does not apply equally to the Senators and/or Representatives." If members of Congress today had to purchase their own retirement plan, pay for college tuition and participate in the healthcare system, maybe different rules for different bills would be passed. It just seems that with all the bad apples, it's hard to find the good ones amongst the bunch.

On August 25, 2018, our country lost a true hero and politician who truly loved his country. Senator John McCain was a different breed. He came from a family of career military officials. He graduated from the Naval Academy in 1958, became a naval aviator, and flew ground-attack aircraft from aircraft carriers during the Vietnam War. He was shot down in October of 1967, captured by the North Vietnamese, and held captive until 1973. The wounds he sustained left him with lifelong physical disabilities, and although he would rather have returned to war like so many of his forefathers, he could not. Instead, he chose a political path, impacting the lives of American citizens as a congressman and then senator for decades, representing Arizona.

John McCain was truly one of a kind. He could be feisty at times and certainly went head-to-head with Trump on many occasions. He was truly bipartisan, and on one of his presidential runs, he actually chose a former Democrat turned independent as his running mate. This bold decision proves what this guy was all about. He was also more faithful to the people of his state of Arizona than to special interest groups. I'm truly hoping that as we watched the coverage of his funeral, all politicians, on both sides of the aisle, took note of this great warrior and proud American.

John McCain's nickname was "Maverick" as he wouldn't always side with his party and would cross the aisle on various issues. As a matter of fact, he would even sit on the other side of the aisle on occasion to demonstrate that he was truly bipartisan. He knew that to accomplish good for America, both sides needed to come together and compromise.

Donald Trump and John McCain certainly locked horns on many occasions. Looking back, with the clear vision of hindsight, I wonder if it was because McCain and Trump had so many similarities that they had issues with one another. It's something to ponder. They were both feisty, outspoken, and stubborn individuals. They both had no political baggage or hidden agendas when seeking office. They both had a clear agenda for the betterment of the American people. That was clearly at the heart of what they sought in their political positions.

While Trump didn't bring any political connections to the White House, he is growing into this new role and developing new relationships along the way. I'd suggest we give him that chance and opportunity.

CHAPTER 4

Everyone Should Have a Nickname

A nickname is a substitute for the proper name of a familiar person, place, or thing. It can be given in affection or ridicule. The nicknames Donald J. Trump has bestowed on others have been in line with the latter. Like him or not, President Trump's style and timing for nicknames is rather entertaining. He doesn't meet with his advisors or PR folks to discuss his thoughts; no, these nicknames are impulsive and fresh. And that's what makes it amusing for me, personally.

I would challenge the reader to come up with a nickname for your best friend, *right now*. Think about it. You've most likely known this person quite well for a number of years. Even so, I'll bet you're struggling to come up with an appropriate and fitting nickname. Trust me. I also tried this exercise and could not produce a witty and fitting moniker. I'm not quite certain how he does it, but on the campaign trail and now in the White House, President Trump certainly has a knack for creating fitting nicknames that stick.

If you don't know this guy has quite the ego, then you truly don't know our president. After all, he spent a number of his years in the entertainment industry and knows how to perform to his audience. Don't try to spar with him (as did Marco Rubio), or you will lose and soon have a nickname of your own. Being a New Yorker and born in Queens, President Donald J. Trump will tell it like it is—whether you want to hear it or not—and tweet his opinion of you to the whole world. He'll even award you a nickname as he kicks you out the door.

I'm not so sure that he does this to be mean but, rather, for the attention. These attention-grabbing names are something he knows the media will latch on to. Though Trump has never said he is at war with the media, the media has said he is at war with them. In my humble opinion, he is playing them like a fine violin. Incredible. So, let's take a peek at some of the nicknames we've come to know over the president's first twenty months in office and while he was on the campaign trail:

Hillary Clinton: Crooked Hillary, Lyin' Hillary, and Heartless Hillary

James Comey: Leakin' James Comey, Sanctimonious James Comey, Slippery James
Kim Jong-un: Rocket Man, Little Rocket Man
Jerry Brown: Governor Jerry "Moonbeam" Brown
Jeb Bush: Low-Energy Jeb
George H. W. Bush: Bush Original
Marco Rubio: Little Marco
Joe Biden: Crazy Joe Biden
Bashar al-Assad: Animal Assad, Gas-Killing Animal
Megan Kelly: Crazy Megan
The New York Times: Failing *New York Times*
CNN: Clinton News Network, Very Fake News
Bill Clinton: Wild Bill
Ted Cruz: Lyin' Ted
Conor Lamb: Lamb the Sham
Barack Obama: Cheatin' Obama
Bernie Sanders: Crazy Bernie
Chuck Schumer: Cryin' Chuck, Fake-Tears Schumer
Nancy Pelosi: MS-13 Lover Nancy Pelosi
Elizabeth Warren: Pocahontas
Robert De Niro: Punchy
John Brennan: Partisan Hack
Corey Booker: Spartacus
Democrats: Party of Crime
Stormy Daniels: Horse Face
Joe Biden: Sleepy Joe
Michael Cohen: Rat
MS-13: Animals

I would suggest that the reader research the specific history of each one of these nicknames. These are quite entertaining to me personally, especially to see how quickly and impulsive he is, President Trump has a craft for sure. The Robert De Niro nickname of "Punchy" was given to De Niro within ten hours after his rant of "F*** Trump" at the Tony Awards on June 11, 2018. For the record, my dad's nickname was "Moose," and my nickname (from Animal, I might add) was "Rizzo, the Italian Knight." And, if my sister is reading this book, her nickname, "Dee Dee," was *not* because I couldn't say Terry. So, yes, we had fake news back in those days as well.

I did a little online research and came across a web page that listed "fifteen hilarious nicknames Donald Trump has been called." What's so hilarious to me is that I'd never heard any of them. Where did these even come from, and who/what was the original source? We certainly know the source of the nicknames I mention above, and I'm certain you have heard well over half of them over and over again.

Here are a few of the more entertaining nicknames for Donald Trump that I'll bet you've never heard before. In parenthesis, I list the originator of the nickname:

Cheeto Jesus (Rick Wilson)
Angry Creamsicle (Stephen Colbert)
Captain Chaos (NBC journalists)
Screaming Carrot Demon (Samantha Bee)
The Tangerine Tornado (Dana Carvey)

There was a total list of fifteen and I didn't recognize or ever hear *any* of them. Maybe it's just me, but if someone calls you a nickname once, it hardly becomes a nickname. It has to stick and become a term of endearment; in contrast, many will recognize and use a real nickname. In this particular case,

I believe that while Donald Trump first came up with the names, it was actually the media that played them over and over again, making them stick. After all, if we take Rocket Man as an example, I believe that Trump said this once, tweeted it once, and maybe brought it up in a speech. Yet, the media played this back so many times you can now purchase Bobbleheads of the president and Rocket Man. Too funny. I believe that we should all take the time to try and come up with a nickname for "The Donald." Oh, wait, he's already had that one for many years!

CHAPTER 5

What American Doesn't Want These Things?

What we have done to the very fabric of our country saddens and truly concerns me. I believe this concern is shared today by nearly all Americans. Our country has now gone so far in both directions—left and right—that few seem to be in the middle. But in 2016, people from all parties came out and elected a president who they truly believed would "Make America Great Again." How can these words be so distasteful to some? In the generations before us, Americans stood together. They loved their country, their family, their flag, their God, and their neighbor. And, they were proud to display affection for the things that mattered most. Look at what's happened today, with a large number of Americans supporting the following:

- Family can be less important than career.
- Illegal immigrants should get more rights, attention, and affection than homeless or addicted citizens.
- Other religious beliefs can be put ahead of our own.
- American flags can be disrespected or not allowed to be displayed in schools.

While I am a Facebook user, I never go on political rants, but many do—whether on the right or the left. Our country is more divided today than I recall in my entire lifetime. I would truly love to hear what some of our forefathers would think about Black Lives Matter, Antifa, Women's March, and other movements that seem to be motivated by hatred.

In another round of protests, players in the NFL took a knee during our national anthem. While at dinner with my nineteen-year-old daughter, I brought up the topic. An NFL owner had stated, "We can't have inmates running the prison," and I wondered what she thought about the situation. She said, "Dad, this is actually the most peaceful protest I have seen." You know what? She's absolutely right!

However, their messaging gets lost. With all of the millions of dollars the NFL players are making and the ultimate power they have, their messaging has fallen way short, and this is why Americans are frustrated with these antics. The follow-the-leader mentality creates a mob scene that becomes rather ugly if examined.

Take, for example, the first Women's March, held January 23, 2017, soon after Trump took office. Madonna stated, "Yes, I have thought an awful lot about blowing up the White House." For me, immediately, the message was lost. Where were these same women over the previous eight years? What was their messaging then? Why did they embrace anger and hatred at the newly elected president, not even in office for one month? Instead of organized events with clear messaging (i.e., "Make America Great Again"), I see a lot of hatred and disrespect for a single individual who is the leader of the most powerful country on the planet today.

In one of Bill O'Reilly's books, he states that he never owned a smartphone as he thought that would be the death of us all. He saw the younger generation relying on text messaging as their primary communication tool and feared interpersonal skills would be lost. Fast-forward to today's Congress. Is texting overriding face-to-face discussions today? Why must each party vote straight down the party line? What happened to the days of going across the street to the pub and working out your differences? Today, it would appear that food fights in Congress are more the norm than a visit to the local pub.

As Americans, we didn't elect a person; we elected a healing and reform process, a process that would fix generations of mistakes. For those who thought everything was fine the way it was, you're probably upset with *any* proposed changes. Here's an analogy I think is fitting: if a person is getting a free newspaper every day and this perk is suddenly taken away, he'd likely be upset. Likewise, those benefitting from social programs like free healthcare, welfare, Medicaid, food stamps and other programs, meet any proposed changes with great resistance.

Let's examine the Social Security program which we continue to hear will go broke by 2034, only sixteen years from now. If I've worked since I was sixteen and paid into the Social Security system for forty-four years yet die before I see the first dollar of benefit, why should others who paid in less and live longer receive more? Pretty simply put, it looks like I am subsidizing others with my contributions. That hardly seems fair to me. If I am the guy mowing the lawn, why should the guy sitting on his porch drinking a cold lemonade get paid for my efforts? The same could be said for other programs as well. My simple solution for the Social Security situation would be to treat it as a piggy bank for my family. I work hard and earn for my family, so that seems fair. Wasn't this the original intent of the program that was started in 1935? After all, I pay my good percentage of taxes to the government and would hope that the subsidies paid out to others come from that resource, not my Social Security benefits. If I die, my Social Security benefits should only pay out to those in my family. Sure seems fair to me.

Now let's try to agree on each of the following fixes:

Stronger Border Security. We can discuss the semantics about who is going to pay for the wall and all that crap, but don't we all want stronger border security? And why would we claim this is racial divide? Four of the pilots who took down the Twin Towers on September 11, 2001, were actually trained in our country. All of the hijackers were foreigners. All of them entered the country legally on a temporary visa, mostly tourist visas for six months. Besides the four pilots, all but one of the terrorists entered the United States only once and had been in the country only three to five months before the attacks. Three of four of the pilots were in the United States illegally at the time of the attacks. If our government has issues with these types of visas and access, wouldn't we all agree that stronger border security is a good thing? It just seems that in politics today, we continue to discuss the problem but not go after the root cause in the first place.

We are a very young country and a country of immigrants. The arrival of Christopher Columbus in 1492 started the European colonization of the Americas. In 1776 the United States of America was declared as an independent nation. Our citizens have ancestors who were Irish, English, German, African, French, Italian, and Mexican legal immigrants. These immigrants traveled to the United States to claim a better life for their families and were willing to work hard, the American way. We were a country of manufacturers, whether we built cars, TVs, or homes, and our forefathers and mothers entered into various skilled trades.

In contrast, for more than the last fifteen years, we have outsourced millions of manufacturing jobs overseas. More people than ever are on welfare or taking advantage of other social entitlement programs. Growing up, I was taught a simple principle: if you don't have the money to buy it, don't. How can any American justify bringing in illegal immigrants to our country while teachers are getting less pay, healthcare costs are rising, and the overall financial burden is greater than ever before? Just fix it.

Legal Immigration. Why would any American vote against programs to properly vet immigrants? My son was just thirteen years old when president-elect Trump was running for office. He focused on what the president-elect kept saying about ISIS. For my son, the message was clear: we must create a safer United States of America and defeat ISIS and foreign terrorists. I just don't see good messaging from those *for* illegal immigration.

My grandparents came here from Italy and Germany through the legal processes. They were hardworking immigrants: an electrician, a steelworker, a home typist, and a maid. Although I have an open mind, I am very closed-minded when it comes to this topic. I am a byproduct of hardworking legal immigrants who made the country what it once was. Shame on me to think it could be that way again.

As I write, politicians are voting for illegal immigrants' rights to free healthcare, free education, and more. Simply put, these policies and politicians are creating virtual billboards advertising to illegal immigrants. One can understand why these problems exist today, but the question is, when will it be fixed? It seems the more bureaucracy created around these issues for vetting legal immigration status and process, the more complicated the problem becomes. We need a lean process in place to fix this. Ultimately, the issue boils down to this: do you want people here legally or illegally? Politicians encouraging foreigners to break our laws doesn't make any sense to me. Just fix it.

Sanctuary Cities. Because I'd never heard this term until recently, I looked up the definition: "refers to municipal jurisdictions, typically in North America and Europe, that limit their cooperation with the national government's effort to enforce immigration law." The leaders of sanctuary cities want to reduce the fear of deportation among people who are in the country illegally. The thought is that immigrants who feel safe will be more willing to report crimes, use health and social services, and enroll their children in school. In the United States, municipal policies include prohibiting police or city employees from questioning people about their immigration status and refusing requests by national immigration authorities to detain people beyond their release date if they are jailed for breaking local law. The Federation for American Immigration Reform[1] estimated in 2018 that more than five hundred US jurisdictions, including states and municipalities, had adopted sanctuary policies. As Americans, we should care about three things when it comes to this topic:

- Are the immigrants here in the United States legally?
- Have they committed any violent crimes against US citizens?
- If these criminals were not in our country illegally, wouldn't we avoid the victimization of our citizens and the costs associated with their crimes, which are paid by American taxpayers?

The Pew Research Institute created a report in 2014 which stated there were 11,200,000 illegal residents residing in the United States at that time. Six states were responsible for 59 percent of this population. Research conducted by the federal government oversight organization Judicial Water in 2014 documents that 50 percent of all federal crimes were committed near our border with Mexico. Here are a few more stats, which don't seem to be on cable news channels when the topic of illegal immigrants is discussed:

---

1   Federation for American Immigration Reform – FAIR is a nonprofit organization seeking to reduce both legal and illegal immigration. It was founded January 2, 1979, and is based in Washington DC (www.fairus.org).

- US Department of Justice (DOJ), 2014: 19 percent or greater (12,000) criminal cases filed by prosecutors were for violent crimes; over 22 percent (13,300) cases were for drug-related felonies.
- US Sentencing Commission, 2014, found that 75 percent of all criminal defendants who were convicted and sentenced for federal drug offenses were illegal immigrants.
- Jointly, the DOJ and Sentencing Commissions found illegal immigrants were convicted and sentenced for over 13 percent of all crimes.
- According to the FBI, 22 percent of all murders committed between 2003 and 2009 were by illegal immigrants.
- In California, nearly one quarter of the nation's undocumented immigrants reside, where they constitute more than 6 percent of the state's population.
- In New York, over three times as many illegal immigrants (or 169) are imprisoned for crimes per one hundred thousand as compared to only forty-eight citizens and legal noncitizen immigrants.

The point I am making is quite simple and is based on my evaluation of these facts. While illegal immigrants make up less than 3.5 percent of the total population in the United States, they are responsible for over 13 percent of all crimes—many violent. This is quite disproportional and *should be of concern to every American today.* Politicians across our great country are actually encouraging citizens to break laws. Just fix it.

Stronger Military. The old adage "peace through strength" applies here. I'm not a proponent of war whatsoever, but trying to put someone in a "time-out" here doesn't always work. If diplomacy doesn't work, resorting to military action might be the only means to complete our mission. I'm not an expert on military affairs by any means and only hope those in charge will do the right thing and make the right choices. It would appear to me that sometimes leaving the bad guy in power is the right thing. (Weren't things better in Iraq when Saddam Hussein was in charge?)

Many bad actors run various countries, and we must deal with each of these threats. I believe our show of force near the Korean peninsula is the factor bringing Rocket Man to the negotiations table. We must remember that our country is just 242 years old while many of these foes have thousands of years of history. That's thousands of years of potential hate and different worldviews that we are not able to identify with. That said, we need military experts and consultants from these foreign lands who might lead us to diplomacy with these dangerous regions of the world.

Stronger military doesn't just mean tanks, planes, aircraft carriers, and subs. It also means investing in artificial intelligence for the military, like drones and other technology to combat terrorists. For the first time in my lifetime, terrorists have brought the battlefield to our soil. Since the younger generation of fighters is most likely communicating via cellphone technology, internet, and other means, we need our largest technology players to get on board and not put political correctness ahead of safety. This means Apple, Facebook, Google, Amazon, and others need to share information with our government when lives are at risk. If someone is on a terrorist watch list, for example, let's work with these large companies to infiltrate and potentially shut down the enemy's source of communication. More common sense, please.

While I can google and rather quickly identify a recipe for chili, I shouldn't be able to google and find "building your own bomb" data. Why is this information easily available while other data might be shut down? Did you know that Amazon is linking explosive recipes by their algorithm, suggesting "frequently bought together"? Really? I do not understand why every American wouldn't want to support strategies to build a stronger military. Just fix it.

US-Based Manufacturing. I'm in the electronics manufacturing sector and have worked in this space since 1980, nearly forty years now. I've had my own business for twenty-five years. I recall a conversation with some buddies on one of my trips to Baltimore. We were watching a football game on a large-screen TV at Eddie's house. In typical Dundalk fashion, everyone was loud and passionate about the problems at hand. We were discussing the Great Recession of 2008, and Johnny yelled, "We should shut down our borders and buy nothing but American." Kevin chimed in, "Yeah, let's do it." The rants and roars continued for about ten minutes or so, and Johnny turned to me and said, "Frank, you're 'Joe College' and being awfully quiet throughout this discussion. Why?"

I chimed in with my bluntly honest opinion and said, "You're all full of crap . . . You're enjoying this fifty-five-inch flat-screen LED TV, right? What about your smartphone? Enjoy your washer? Dryer?" Johnny said, "Yeah. So, what's your point?" I retorted, "We don't make any of this stuff in America anymore, including the light bulbs. If it weren't for

Chinese and offshore manufacturing, we'd be sitting here in the dark!"

Here I was, with five of my closest old-neighborhood buddies who had no clue that all this stuff was made offshore. Many people don't; kids today certainly don't realize the repercussions of foreign dependence on manufactured goods. Everyone wants to have an iPhone, but few realize Apple doesn't manufacture *a single product* in the United States. Apple is the ninth largest company in the world, yet they don't make a single product in the United States, where the company was founded.

The personal computer was invented by IBM in my town, Boca Raton, but all associated manufacturing is long gone now. Motorola, Intel, Tyco, Jabil, and so many others have laid off thousands upon thousands of workers here in the United States, only to open factories in China, Hungary, Poland, Brazil, Mexico, Costa Rica, and other regions that offer cheap labor resources.

In 1982 I bought my first IBM PC for four thousand dollars. You can buy a laptop today for two hundred dollars. While the price of other goods (homes, cars, gas, a gallon of milk) has increased in cost, why did TVs, computers, and electronics drop in price by ten to twenty times? Does that make sense to you? What happened to being proud about "Made in America"? Some of you might be too young to remember when "Made in Japan" meant poor quality.

If we continue to outsource our manufacturing jobs, we will continue to outsource our children's futures. With manufacturing facilities come opportunities for engineers, accountants, skilled laborers, and others. I'll ask this question: how many of you know a kid, saddled with debt, who finished at least four years of college yet cannot get a job in her field of study? I've known many young adults in this tough spot, and this trend is concerning and sad. I was fortunate to complete college and not only get a job in my field, electrical engineering, but to get a job at the specific company I wanted, Westinghouse in Baltimore. For me, this was the American Dream.

I'm hoping all Americans will believe in bringing the manufacturing plants, hence jobs, back to America. The cost of goods should only increase slightly, as everything is automated today, and these plants will pay dividends in many ways.

To dovetail immigration policies into manufacturing jobs, maybe there is a fast track to legal immigration based upon employment initiatives. Just thinking out loud here. Maybe someone who's much smarter than me can come up with the fine print around such policies.

With decades of outsourcing manufacturing jobs and poor trade deals, we have become wimps at the negotiation table. Like so many other topics and policies, when change in this area is proposed, it is met with great resistance. In our short history, we invented and built things and created a country that became first in so many areas. We invented Hollywood, the transistor radio, the Intel microprocessor, the personal computer, the telegraph, the copy machine, the electric light, and so much more. Why, then, would we be enticed to outsource our latest technologies to Communist countries who are stealing our intellectual property? Just fix it.

Cutting Taxes. On December 22, 2017, President Trump signs the Tax Cuts and Jobs Act. Immediately, companies like AT&T released news that it would give $1,000 bonuses to 200,000 employees. Comcast, Wells Fargo, VISA, and other companies immediately announced employee raises and bonuses. With Nancy Pelosi's net worth at twenty-nine million dollars, it's no wonder she calls one-thousand-dollar bonuses "crumbs" to Americans. While Nancy had her very own Trump Complex moment, remember what I said earlier. When there is no filter and comments are spontaneous, they are *real*. Nancy absolutely meant what she said here. The government bureaucrats in power today have very high net worths. After all, Nancy is number fifteen on that list. John Kerry's estimated net worth is at $238 million and several current senators have a net worth well over one hundred million dollars. This "swamp" is driving every important decision in our life today.

For me, personally, I'm all for paying more in taxes when I believe in what my government is doing for me. Tax is relative to the amount of income earned. I doubt any of us have problems with paying more if we make more. However, we need a strong economy with more job opportunities and businesses. This will create a domino effect that is good for every single American. Just fix it.

In conclusion, I would think that most, if not all, Americans want these things. Stronger border security, legal immigration, stronger military, more US-based manufacturing, and lower taxes. I'm not certain why we continue to politicize such important issues and go to war with each other over this. Would it really be better if we had no border security, more illegal immigrants, a weaker military, less jobs, and higher taxes? Can we find agreement?

CHAPTER 6

Does Everyone
Need a Time-Out?

I f any of you watch the daily news feeds or are paying any
attention to what the leaders in our great country are
doing today, you are surely scratching your head regarding
the double standards that might exist for career politicians
compared to ourselves. We surely must have too many laws
on the books today because they seem to be broken every day
in our Department of Justice, FBI, Congress, and so forth.
I have a solution. We'll just give everyone a time-out. That's
sure to work in this politically correct world. Suppose a kid

is running around the classroom yelling and screaming and doing everything he possibly can to disrupt the class; what's the solution? Let's take Johnny over to the corner and put him in a time-out. Really? Every day, we see instances within our educational institutions of what our society is doing to our children.

Now, let's fast-forward to take a peek at how these kids behave in society once they are adults. Political opposition has turned into criminal investigations. Everyone should go to jail if you pay any attention, whatsoever, to the daily news. The list of parolees would include James Clapper, Hillary Clinton, Donald Trump, Barak Obama, General David Petraeus, Susan Rice, John Brennan, Michael Flynn, Christopher Wray, the love couple of Peter Strzok and Lisa Page, and, oh, so many more.

Depending on the news network you watch, the list of criminals might vary for sure. The news media has become increasingly bias. Although Fox News is my go-to network, they are hardly "fair and balanced." All networks have become increasingly biased in their reporting and cater to particular audiences that prefer to hear the news reported in a particular way, supporting a specific viewpoint. Just as one party has gone extremely right and one party extremely left, so, too, have the news outlets. What then for those of us in the middle?

When we were kids, punishments were tailored to the issue—a punishment to suit the crime, so to speak. Why, then, does our Congress, as well as the news media, want everyone to go straight to jail? Consider how infractions are handled in schools; punishments might vary from in-school suspension to detention to out of school suspension to expulsion. Different punishments are awarded after considering the specific act.

Why can't we use a graduated system of penalty against our politicians who have sworn to uphold our laws and defend our democracy?

At some point in their careers, public servants swore an oath to defend the very laws that they break themselves today, either flagrantly or without thinking. Regardless of their motives, some type of punishment should be enforced. While I do not believe all of these people should go straight to jail, being of Catholic faith, I do believe in purgatory. Their infractions should go on record so that future generations will realize consequences follow crime. It would appear by today's standards that there is either prosecution or no crime committed whatsoever. I have a very low tolerance for these continued practices and believe we are, once again, applying "trophy generation" rules instead of proper punishment.

Therefore, here are the time-outs I would assign as punishment for current wrongdoings:

> **Hillary Clinton:** Former first lady (1993-2001); US senator (2001-2009); secretary of state (2009-2013); 2008 presidential primary participant (Obama got the party's nomination); and 2016 presidential nominee for the Democratic Party.
>
> Wrongdoings: She committed 18 crimes, including perjury; using the family's private email server for handling classified information while secretary of state (2,093 confidential emails, 110 classified emails, 22 top-secret emails); using Blackberry phone to communicate; tampering with evidence; destroying government property;

participating in Benghazi controversy and Clinton Foundation controversy; private server that was hacked and more.[2]

Time-out: Never, ever allowed to run for any public office or work in any government agency or institution.

James Comey: Seventh director of the FBI from 2013 until his dismissal in May 2017.

Wrongdoings: While holding the top post at the most elite federal law enforcement agency on the planet, whose motto is "Fidelity, Bravery, Integrity," he failed the American people by allowing bias amongst top officials who were handling critical investigations of both Hillary Clinton and Donald J. Trump. He lied under oath to the Senate Committee when he claimed he had never leaked information and never approved a leak. Basically, he demonstrated his own bias.

Time-out: His publisher, Macmillan, should have revoked the $2 million advance and walked away from the book deal. For those who watched his testimony to the Senate Judiciary Committee, we could tell he was posturing for his book with every word spoken and every answer. *A Higher Loyalty* . . . really?

Andrew McCabe: The number two man at the FBI, as deputy director, he worked for the FBI from 1996 until January, 2018. When James

---

2   110 classified emails (Wikipedia), 2,093 confidential emails (US State Dept.), 18 crimes including perjury (House Oversight and Government Reform Committee)

Comey was fired by President Trump, he became the acting director of the FBI for the period from May 9, 2017, until January 29, 2018.

Wrongdoing: He lied to internal investigators for an inspector general report regarding the Hillary Clinton email scandal.

Time-out: The US Government should not pay him his pension after working for the FBI for the twenty-two-year period he served there.

Peter Strzok: He joined the FBI in the 90s, and as an agent he was section chief of the counterespionage section that led a team of a dozen investigators probing Hillary Clinton's use of a personal email server. He rose to the position of deputy assistant director of the counterintelligence division. He led the FBI's investigation into Russian interference in the 2016 election and became the lead investigator for Robert Mueller's special counsel investigation, which was looking for links and possible collusion between the Trump campaign and Russia.

Wrongdoings: He sent hate-fueled text messages against candidate Donald Trump within the FBI while he was a lead prosecutor on the very high-profile cases of Hillary Clinton and Donald Trump. Infamous text messages between Strzok and Lisa Page, legal counsel to Deputy Director Andrew McCabe, became viral. Here's an example of these texts:

PAGE: "[Trump's] not ever going to become president, right? Right?!"

STRZOK: "No. No he won't. We'll stop it."

These two facts get Peter Strzok in even more trouble:

1. His text messaging history on the same subject.
2. His blatant hatred and bias against the person he was investigating.

Another exchange with Page—with whom he was having an extramarital affair at the time—from August 2016 (I'm not making this stuff up):

STRZOK: "I want to believe the path you threw out for consideration in Andy's office—that there's no way he gets elected—but I'm afraid we can't take that risk. It's like an insurance policy in the unlikely event you die before you're forty."

Time-out: Ultimately, Strzok's boss was Donald Trump. I don't know of any job in the United States where you could be so insubordinate to your boss. He was eventually fired, however should not be allowed to work in any government or public service position and should not receive any pension portion from the government. He was insubordinate to the government he served, and therefore the punishment should fit the crime.

As we make decisions regarding such punishments, do we fully understand the implications? We are setting precedence for future generations. Is there no punishment or crime for potentially sharing classified information with foreign agents? Is there no punishment or crime for being insubordinate to your boss? Is there no punishment or crime for lying? If these are the actions taken by the highest officials in our land, what can we expect from our children or their children?

Consequences for bad behavior in public office are imperative. Otherwise, we essentially tell kids that it is acceptable to disrespect teachers or parents. I never cursed in front of one of my parents. At age sixty, I still speak to neighbors where I grew up with respect, as Mr. or Mrs. Today, we can threaten the White House with bombings, show a decapitated effigy of our current president, allow restaurant owners to refuse service to the press secretary, or say, "F@#* Trump!" during the Tony awards. It's amazing that parents are often disgusted by the language used in rap music or YouTube videos their children might be exposed to. However, these kids also watch TV. How can we punish kids for listening to or saying much less than the civic leaders or celebrity personalities on TV? Our children need role models, just as we did. I can't recall such bad behavior by past role models. Now that I ponder the state of things today, I think we might all need a time-out.

Such issues seem to become political footballs whether you sit on the right or left side of the aisle. By not denouncing or criticizing such actions, you are then endorsing such actions by default. On one hand, the Democrats seem to despise every word or action of the current president. Does this make it okay to give such crimes and actions above a pass? Again, this is very confusing to me; therefore, I see mixed messaging. The messaging gets lost for me when there is no punishment for such horrible actions. Everyone should be accountable for their actions. If we elect someone into such a position of power, we wouldn't want them to break laws in order to accomplish their mission. But then again, if we examine some of the actions that I laid out here, we might begin to question what their mission was in the first place and better understand how we have become so divided as a country and a people.

CHAPTER 7

The Impact of Entitlements

Entitlement: belief that one is deserving of or entitled to certain privileges; a government program providing benefits to members of a specified group.

I recall a famous case decided on August 18, 1994. A seventy-nine-year-old woman, Stella Liebeck, sued McDonald's after she suffered third-degree burns in her pelvic region when she accidentally spilled hot coffee in her lap after purchasing it from a McDonald's restaurant. The jury in a New Mexico courtroom awarded her nearly three million dollars; however, she ultimately received six hundred and forty thousand dollars for this lawsuit. Really? Would she have also sued McDonald's if the coffee wasn't hot enough? What happens if a movie goes out for a brief period at a movie theater? Are we all entitled to a refund?

On a hot summer day here in South Florida in June, 2018, I had plans to take my nineteen-year-old daughter to the movies. It was planned as a daddy-daughter date since we couldn't do it on Father's Day. My sixteen-year-old son immediately questioned why he wasn't going to the movies as well. As I have often taken both children to the movies, together, my son felt a sense of entitlement. He felt he deserved a movie outing, too. How did we arrive at this place where we all feel so entitled to anything and everything? Maybe it's not the best example, but I hope this example underscores the pickle we are in as a wave of entitlements has swept our country.

It seems both key political parties politicize various social programs and even laws. As I write, our country faces polarizing illegal immigration issues. Children are heart-wrenchingly separated from their parents after crossing our borders illegally. But this particular situation has been brewing for a while. Former presidents have allowed illegal immigration, essentially allowing noncitizens to break our laws for years. By not enforcing these laws, we created a sense of entitlement among those hoping to immigrate. I am dumbfounded when the media and the liberals attack the current president for enforcing our border and immigration laws. I lose respect for those who would favor allowing such laws to be broken.

I'm certainly not a politician. The closest I've come to understanding a political environment was when I was the vice president of a homeowners association. My approach—

and the advice I received from a board member in another community—was to enforce all rules and regulations, *making no exceptions*. If a rule was unpopular, one should write a new one and put it to a vote. Seems like common sense to me. How, then, can career politicians be so naïve to allow national laws to be broken? Again, if you don't like the law, write a new one and vote on it.

You see, when we take things away from people who have been getting those very things for years for free, major uproar ensues. Welfare is a good example. Generations of families have received welfare. Therefore, they now feel entitled to this money. Why aren't we doing more root-cause analysis to figure out how to get these families off of welfare and prevent others from going on welfare in the first place? The same logic applies to illegal border crossings, free healthcare, and other social programs. By offering such entitlement programs, we created a population that will strike back when we try to roll back social aid.

I suppose I grew up in a different era as I never felt entitled to anything. If I wanted better, I knew I had to work for it. I was raised in a lower-middle-income neighborhood where my first bicycle was my older brother's hand-me-down. When raised this way, one often develops a can-do attitude about achievement and success.

Please don't have misguided anger tantrums over the current president because he is trying to solve these very problems and enforcing the laws of the land. Remember, he didn't write all these laws; he's simply suggesting we enforce them as written. Why is there such hatred for the president? It is as if some believe every action he takes is to destroy us. Although his famous slogan is, "Make America Great Again," it really should be, "Make *the Next American Generations* Great Again."

I'm not a political historian, but I believe actions taken today might not be felt or understood for many years, possibly decades, to come. Just as in business, we might not feel the impact of decisions until some much later time. Change is often painful at first, but we need to change our overall behavior and attitudes regarding such entitlements, and this must start at the top. The changes we make today are making things better for future generations. Let's not have tantrums and protests every time things don't seem to go our way. Let's not feel so entitled. After all, it's the "everyone gets a trophy generation" folks who have never been taught about losing. Entitlement is what they know because of systems put in place in years past. Is anyone reflecting on that fact?

Recently, regarding families crossing into the country illegally, elected officials have claimed we should abolish Immigrations and Customs Enforcement (ICE). Such tirades continue to baffle me, yet I try to examine each of these topics thoroughly. First, ICE agents are not separating children from parents at the border. It is our border control agents actually enforcing the laws. They don't rewrite their job description after they get the job.

I suggest handling such important issues the same way we might handle issues in our families: have a sit-down meeting, family conference, or dinner, and try to work out the differences, taking time to understand each side. Both sides must be good listeners. I can assure you that if one of my kids was trying to get my attention by protesting on my front lawn for all the neighbors to see, the outcome would be very different than if we had a proper discussion. It seems that for every issue facing our country today, the media outlets pour gasoline on these fires and douse the flames.

Everything in life is a negotiation, and both sides must be willing to compromise to get to an end point. Regarding entitlements, we must teach kids how to lose as much as we teach them how to win. Handling the stress and anxiety that comes with loss will prepare these future leaders for the inevitable setbacks that happen to us all. As I learned many years ago in my own business dealings with customers, you can find acceptable ways to say no while still holding your ground.

Entitlement programs in the United States today are basically social programs or welfare subsidies. Such programs include cash assistance, healthcare and medical provisions, food assistance, housing subsidies, energy and utility subsidies, education and childcare assistance, and subsidies and assistance for other basic services. These programs impact our society in two basic areas, one financial and the other emotional:

1. Financial Impact: Funding for assistance and subsidization programs comes from the American taxpayer.

2. Emotional Impact: The legal taxpayer has been watching her utility bills, healthcare, housing, rent, and other costs increase. Her bills increase because others are paying nothing or the government is paying fixed, reduced costs for such things; thus, the expense is defrayed by increasing costs for the taxpayer. The emotional toll of this process is seen in the anger American workers feel. They are working overtime

to make ends meet with less time with their families, while others who might not work at all get everything for free.

To put entitlement in proper perspective, consider this: as of August, 2018, more jobs are available than people on food stamps. Think about that fact. So, despite all the recent job claims, food stamp recipients are still at recession-era levels. As of 2017, there were 42.6 million Americans on food stamps. This number is down 2 million under President Trump, however this figure still represents 13 percent of all Americans who are on food stamps today. We can analyze the Supplemental Nutrition Assistance Program (SNAP) data and the percentage of citizens receiving food stamps until the cows come home, but the reality is that once people receive entitlements, or free stuff, it's really hard to take it away.

I'm reminded of a recent comparison of two Democrats, John F. Kennedy and Alexandria Ocasio-Cortez, the twenty-eight-year-old democratic socialist congresswoman recently elected in New York. John F. Kennedy stated in 1961, "My fellow Americans, ask not what your country can do for you, ask what you can do for your country." Compare that position to the popular position of Alexandria Ocasio-Cortez: "We have a political culture of intimidation, of favoring, of patronage, and of fear, and that is no way for a community to be governed." Alexandria Ocasio-Cortez supports and believes in free stuff.

Undoubtedly, when I was in my late teen years and early twenties, with zero responsibility, free stuff was cool. But we should all know by now that nothing in life is free. Take a look at what's going on in Venezuela today. The country has declined since the days of President Hugo Chavez in 2010 to President Nicolas Maduro today. Maduro has served since 2013. I'm not so certain that Alexandria Ocasio-Cortez is paying attention to this important time in history for that socialist country:

- Massive currency devaluation on August 17, 2018, *slashed five zeros* off their crippled bolivar currency.
- Venezuela faces 60,000 percent inflation.
- A stack of money is needed to buy a bag of rice; how about three hundred thousand bolivars for an iPhone 6? This is equivalent to $47,250 US dollars.
- Minimum wage increased to the equivalent of twenty-eight dollars an hour, or thirty-four times the previous levels.
- International Monetary Fund predicts Venezuela's inflation will be at 100,000,000 percent this year.
- Oil production accounts for 96 percent of their revenue and slipped to a thirty-year low of 1.4 million barrels per day as opposed to 3.2 million barrels a day ten years ago.
- 2,300,000 Venezuelans have fled their country since 2014.

We must learn to take responsibility for our mistakes, correct the wrongdoings of the past, and not jeopardize future generations because of our missteps. I can't help but feel that any politician who would want "free" things, knowing that they are not really free at all, is either naïve, trying to get votes, or stupid. I never expected a free house, free car, free college education, or even a free meal. I believe that there are two types of people that inhabit this world: people who lead and people who need to be led. For the people who need to be led, I point the blame squarely at those politicians that are not examining the root-cause and truly addressing these problems today. America's poor, homeless, addicted, and sick need the leaders of this great country to make the right decisions and lead.

I believe the leaders of our country need to be prudent with decisions they make on entitlements and think about the real harm they might be bringing to generations of families in the future. These feel-good strategies are sure to win votes in the election booths. But we need to be smart to realize most, if not all, of these platform positions are espoused to win votes. Politicians know better, and it truly saddens me that those who need to be led are being taken advantage of. Politicians promoting entitlement policies are actually seeking to saddle future generations with more debt. Nothing in life is free. Can we try to work together to figure out how to truly address these problems today?

CHAPTER 8

The Art of the Deal

My career spans thirty-seven years, with well over thirty-five years spent selling capital equipment. There is certainly an art to selling electronic assembly and test equipment that can cost hundreds of thousands of dollars to a prospective company. Earlier in my career, I attended many sales training programs, including Wilson Counselor Selling, Karrass Effective Negotiating, Holden Sales Techniques, and other programs designed to hone my skills in this area. I spent thousands of dollars on special sales training tapes that I would listen to while traveling hundreds of miles in my car to the next town's appointments.

However, strategic selling skills are but one piece of the puzzle. Product knowledge, research on the competition, an understanding of your audience, past successes, and simple "gut instinct" are other important elements.

As I've shared, the closest I ever came to politics was serving on the board of directors for a residential community. For a large telecommunications agreement, I was the person heading the team doing all the technical evaluations and ultimate contract negotiations. In the final stages of preparation, I prepared a spreadsheet that had the key variables for a contract negotiation with input from each of the board members for his position on that particular topic. With only three of the seven board members attending the final negotiation meeting, there would not be a quorum.

The three of us met for breakfast at a local restaurant, and one board member said to me, "Do you really think they will agree to these terms?" My response was, "How do we know what they will agree to if we don't ask?" In the end, the vendor agreed to all of our requested terms. The lesson learned here was that having inexperienced people conducting very important negotiations whereby they have had no prior experience could suffer very bad consequences.

In politics, as well as in media, many have law degrees or a background in law. I'm certainly not picking on lawyers; they have their rightful place and purpose in our society. But, isn't bringing in the lawyers the last resort in a negotiation?

When I was a board member, none of my prior background, experience, or educational history prepared me for that job. To a much greater degree, this is precisely how politics works today. A governed body writes the laws and enforces them for a community. I contend that it's the politicians of today who have demonstrated that they don't have a clue and cannot get anything done. Is this the reason that so many of us have voted for those that are not career politicians today? Do we think donors and lobbyists are lining the pockets of career politicians? How is it that all these guys got so rich in the first place?

After years of bad deals in recent history, it seems that Americans wanted a dealmaker in Washington, an experienced dealmaker with a knack for making the right decisions and whose gut instincts have been more right than wrong. Not every decision by every dealmaker is going to be the right one, but remember what we learned from Thomas Peters's *In Search of Excellence*: if ten decisions need to be made, it's better to make ten decisions, even if only eight of the ten are the right decisions. We can live with the two wrong decisions, which is still a better outcome than only making six of the ten decisions. Follow?

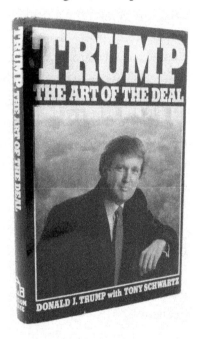

It seems to me more books are in the future for politicians than good deals for American families. Posturing, getting your name in the papers, and other stunts seem to be the driving force for a good number of politicians today. If someone has a school project due or a test on a particular day, she prepares. Why, then, when we have a budget to pass and a potential government shutdown looming are there eleventh-hour shenanigans before finally getting things done? Why wasn't the important homework handled beforehand? Why doesn't our Congress meet its deadlines and commitments for the American people? Very few of our political leaders have experience in consummating a big deal, yet they are engaged in them all the time.

We finally have a dealmaker (or breaker) in Washington DC, but every time a deal is about to be consummated, great resistance appears from one party. Everything doesn't have to be turned into a science project or procrastinated over for years. We need to get the job done. We need to make decisions, cut the deal, and get to the next deal.

Everyone is certainly entitled to their opinion regarding our new president, and everyone has one for sure. However, no matter what one might think, we should not undervalue or underestimate his business savvy, experience, and success. With more than five hundred businesses organized under the Trump brand and billions of dollars of net worth, I would hardly call him a slouch. It is fair to have constructive criticism for various deals and decisions, but we should also know that we are not dealing with someone who has a history of bad decisions.

This new dealmaker in Washington offers fresh perspective and certainly a nonpolitical perspective. Decisions are not made to satisfy any particular political group or lobbyist so much as they are made to appease the American people and follow through on the promises he made on the campaign trail. So many things are broken in America today that we should trust this fixer is on our side. He's preached a pro-American, pro-me, and a pro-you agenda since taking office. Let's trust his instincts and dealmaking abilities as I'm certain future history books will show he was one of the best presidents in American history. Donald Trump is not attempting to enrich himself as he's already wealthy. The decisions and deals he makes today are to enrich *all* Americans, not the top 1 percent.

I truly look forward to the before and after comparisons of the Trump presidency to see what accomplishments were made. Then we can thank him—and his family for allowing him—for supporting the future of my children and their children for a much better America. How is it that other world powers who attended the United Nations meetings in late September, 2018, are more supportive of his positions and policies than nearly half of Americans? Simply put, other nations are not in the crisis mode of great division that grips America.

Again, multibillionaire dealmakers aren't looking for popularity. They've already succeeded. Consider the example of Bill Gates. He was just a computer software developer when he visited IBM in Boca Raton in the early 80s and made history. Bill Gates pressed the IBM execs to allow him to own the rights to the software operating system he would write for them, famously named "Windows." They gladly complied, thinking all the real money would be made in the hardware anyway. Now, Bill Gates is one of the richest men in the world. As a comparison, for reference, Microsoft Corporation is worth $560 billion today, and IBM is worth $138 billion. All I can say is wow. But who saw this coming at that time? These individuals are also in the billionaire's club: Elon Musk, Bill Gates, Wayne Huzienga (Alamo Car Rental, Blockbuster Video, Waste Management, AutoNation). Are we really going to second-guess those who build such successful empires? Really? Not me.

If all past deals America has made were good deals, we wouldn't be at nearly $21 trillion of debt. If our new dealmaker—or breaker—decides to renegotiate prior bad trade deals, why wouldn't we trust him? After all, he has more experience at business negotiations than many others around him or in Congress. If Trump decides to get up from a negotiation table, cancel a critical meeting, or send messages to the media, I will certainly not second-guess his strategy. When were things ever so crystal clear to all Americans about how to deal with China, Mexico, or Canada regarding trade deals?

In business, I have certainly witnessed products that flopped. However, two things have been very clear: one, the company must always give the product support and a chance; and two, the end customer ultimately decides whether it's a hit or a flop. In our current political climate, Americans are quick to pass judgment on extremely critical deals—deals that could have an enormous impact on our national debt. I'm sure if we look back in history, the iPhone wasn't an immediate success on Day 1. As a matter of fact, there is quite the history. Apple introduced the iPOD for storing and playing music. Steve Jobs was concerned about phones that were also able to play music so they did a collaboration with Motorola to develop a product called ROKR E1 that could play iTunes. The product was horrible and Apple realized they had to develop their own phone. The point is that products, like deals, may change and evolve over time based on the direct impact to the end user. In the case of all political decisions, Americans are the end user.

Just as in the case of any war, it's very hard to predict how long the discord might last. How many casualties will be realized? What will be gained in the end? Just as we shouldn't share war strategies ahead of time, I don't believe we should be sharing and discussing all the details of such intricate trade deals either. Both sides must feel as if they have won something. I only hope the master negotiator is sitting on our side of the table, not theirs.

After five hundred days in office, Trump had accomplished more than past presidents:

- 94 meetings with world leaders
- 250 calls with world leaders and heads of state
- 11 direct interactions with Vladimir Putin
- 180 bills signed into laws
- 192 flights on Air Force One
- 14 foreign countries visited
- 3,496 presidential tweets for transparency

Besides these accomplishments, Trump also deserves respect for these deals and decisions:

- He enforced Obama's "red line" against Syria.
- He approved a $47 million arms package for Ukraine, sent troops to Poland's border, and imposed new sanctions on Moscow for violating the Intermediate-Range Nuclear Forces Treaty.
- He recognized Jerusalem as Israel's capital and moved the US Embassy from Tel Aviv to Jerusalem.
- He withdrew from the Paris Agreement to combat climate change.

- He got NATO allies to kick in $12 billion more toward our collective security.
- He has virtually eliminated the Islamic State's physical caliphate.
- He admitted he was wrong on Afghanistan and reversed Obama's disastrous withdrawal there.
- He enacted historic tax and regulatory reform.
- He installed two conservative judges who will preside for decades.
- He renegotiated the NAFTA deal with Mexico and Canada under a new name.

Love him or hate him, Donald Trump co-wrote the book, *The Art of the Deal* in 1987, and as Americans we are getting to watch this play out before our very eyes. If such master negotiators make up less than 1% of the people, why would 50% want to second guess the less than 1% on their deal making strategies? These movers and shakers are a rare breed, for sure, and they have a knack for winning and winning strategies. The best dealmakers know that every deal dies three times before it closes. Let's be a bit patient before we pass judgment.

CHAPTER 9

The Element of Surprise

The most remarkable leaders in the world are tough and unpredictable. This is true for the leaders of such powerful countries as Russia, China, Japan, Israel, and Saudi Arabia, to name a few. During Donald Trump's campaign, he repeatedly had said that the United States can no longer be the world's policeman. It's rather interesting some of the strong comments that were made coupled with some of his actions to date.

Meanwhile, Trump has given more power to his military leaders, and one never really knows what his next move might be. This element of surprise gives great power to this world leader. Do we really need blueprints and documented withdrawal strategies like our past leaders provided? We are the most transparent society in the world and have tended to share everything with both our allies as well as our adversaries.

The Syrian dictator Bashar al-Assad launched a chemical weapons airstrike on April 4, 2017. The release of the toxic gas, which included sarin, killed at least seventy-four people and injured more than 557. The attack was the deadliest use of chemical weapons in the Syrian Civil War since the Ghouta chemical attack in 2013. In retaliation for this attack, without hesitation and after meeting with his military leaders, President Trump responded with an attack on April 7, 2017. We launched fifty-nine Tomahawk Land Attack Missiles at the Shavrat Airbase and a Syrian airfield.

Until such time that we dropped the Mother of all Bombs (MOAB), technical name GBU-43/B Massive Ordnance Air Blast, in Afghanistan, I didn't even know such a weapon existed. The most powerful nonnuclear weapon in our arsenal, it was delivered by a C-130 plane on April 13, 2017, on an ISIL tunnel complex in that country. This was the first operational use of that bomb, which had first been developed in 2003. This strike killed ninety-four ISIS-K militants, including four commanders. A weapon of intimidation and a unit cost of $170,000, the bomb weighs 21,600 pounds and was specifically designed for the type of terrains we went after that day in the ISIS mission.

After numerous threats to the dictator of North Korea, Kim Jong-un—including, "My button is bigger than your button"; "You will see fire and fury like the world has never known"; and "You will suffer the same fate as Muammar Gaddafi if you don't denuclearize"—the media was having a field day, and we were all on the edge of our seats. Kim Jong-un was firing test missiles over Japan and doing some very provocative military exercises to threaten the United States. However, Trump became the first sitting president ever to meet face-to-face with the leader of North Korea when a summit occurred on June 12, 2018, in Singapore.[3] The contents of the meeting between the president and supreme leader of North Korea had not been released to the public at the time of this writing.

Just last week, however, fifty-five cases of remains of US soldiers were returned from North Korea after sixty-eight years. Certainly, this is a positive first step and part of the commitments that were made by Kim Jong-un at the summit. It will take months for DNA testing to confirm the identities and determine whether, in fact, these are the remains of US troops.

The Iran nuclear deal between the Islamic Republic of Iran and a group of world powers was reached in 2015 under President Barack Obama. The world powers included the permanent members of the United Nations Security Council, United States, United Kingdom, Russia, France, and China, plus Germany and the European Union. In August of 2016, President Obama had flown $1.8 billion in cargo planes to Iran as part of the deal.

After threatening to do so for the better part of a year and on his campaign trail, President Trump announced that the United States was withdrawing from the Joint Comprehensive Plan of Action Agreement that was executed in 2015. The announcement was made on May 8, 2018. At midnight on August 6, 2018, sanctions against Iran were restored. Within

---

3   Mark Landler, *The New York Times*, May 24, 2018.

the first week of August, 2018, President Trump stated he would meet with President Rouhani of Iran without any preconditions. Suffice it to say that President Rouhani was having temper tantrums over reimposed sanctions and the United States' withdrawal from the agreement. Time will tell what happens, but if you examine the history between President Trump and "Rocket Man" during 2017, one could never have imagined a summit would take place or that test missiles being fired over Japan and threats to Guam would cease.

In my own tiny space, I also have found that toes-to-toes negotiations and face-to-face meetings are necessary to reach the endgame. In any large-deal negotiation, gut instinct and experience come into play for sure. While Donald J. Trump has had zero past experience in military strategies, tactics, and meetings, he seems to have surrounded himself with the best of the best to confront such issues.

While I truly appreciate the element of surprise and see significant advantages to such tactics, I continue to be concerned with the Democratic Party's dislike of this president and every tactical move he makes, the continued leaks to the press, and the overall transparency we provide with such delicate matters. You can research the number and types of munitions, the number of planes or military bases—everything funded by taxpayer dollars. The irony is that we don't have the same information about the enemy. How many nukes does Kim Jong-un have? Where are they? Why would we continue to be so transparent with our tactics, strategies, and intelligence if we want to win wars? By sharing this data, aren't we informing our enemies of the munitions and military arsenal they will require to defeat us? Wouldn't this be the same as a coach in the NFL sharing his playbook before the big game with the competing coach? It's above my pay grade, but I just don't get it.

In my business, the most dangerous competitor is the one you know the least about. Again, I'm small potatoes, but I think the element of surprise gives us great strength and power. I'm not all for dropping bombs and blowing up the bad guys; I believe all diplomatic strategies should be exercised first. However, history does show that the bad guys hang out together and go to each other's birthday parties. I'm certain they all share their views and strategies for taking down the United States. Remember, we're the youngest guy in the room. Many of these countries have thousands of years of history compared to our 242-year history. And much hatred is directed toward our civilization and what we stand for.

CHAPTER 10

"The Star-Spangled Banner"

The famous War of 1812 began with America's simmering anger toward the British for interfering in American trade, forcing Americans to join in the Royal Navy, and standing in the way of westward expansion. We declared war in June, 1812, but British forces were distracted as they had another ongoing war with France at the time. Hence, we declared some early victories, earned as a byproduct of their distractions. But after Napoleon's defeat at the Battle of Waterloo in April, 1814, the British turned their full attention to the war in North America. That August, the British troops invaded Washington DC and set fire to the Capitol and other government buildings. The Royal Navy then turned its sights onto the key seaport in Baltimore, Maryland, about eight miles from where I was raised.

On September 13, 1814, US soldiers endured twenty-five hours of British bombardment at Baltimore's Fort McHenry. Early that next morning, US troops hoisted a huge American flag over the fort, marking a crucial victory and a turning point in the war. While anchored on a ship in Baltimore's harbor, Francis Scott Key wrote "The Star-Spangled Banner" to capture the thrill of seeing "the broad stripes and bright stars" still "gallantly streaming" the morning after battle. It became our country's national anthem in 1931 after more than a century of being one of America's most popular patriotic tunes. Francis Scott Key actually wrote four original verses; however, only one is commonly sung today. It wasn't until the Civil War, some forty-seven years later, that the song became popular as it gained a deeper meaning when the American flag became an increasingly powerful symbol of *national unity.*

"The Star-Spangled Banner" made its official sporting debut on September 5, 1918, during the first World Series game between the Chicago Cubs and the Boston Red Sox. The song was played during the seventh-inning stretch. So, for a hundred years now, the national anthem has been played at thousands of sporting events in the United States. Two things really bother most Americans when it comes to our national anthem: one, singers who spin or alter the song, whether by melody or lyrics; and two, when professional players take a knee, wave their fists, turn their backs, or otherwise disrespect the flag, our national anthem, and what they stand for.

Though I'm generally not impressed when singers spin the song a bit differently, two notable artists have done our national anthem justice. Whitney Houston, who gets lots of accolades for one of the best renditions of our national anthem at Super Bowl XXV in Tampa, 1991, and my personal all-time favorite rendition by lesser-known rock band Madison Rising. I encourage you to google the YouTube video for the latter as it is certain to give you goose bumps.

As for players taking a knee, I do not understand our highest-paid entertainers showing such disrespect for the very flag and country that allows them to earn such salaries and enjoy the NFL, which only exists in our America. Just this year, Aaron Rogers of the Green Bay Packers signed a $134 million, four-year deal. Matt Ryan of the Atlanta Falcons signed for a $33 million salary. There were eleven other contracts signed for over $22 million each. The NFL's top ten players in 2018 will earn a combined $424 million in salaries, bonuses, endorsements and licensing income. Is this "sick money" creating spoiled brats? To put this in perspective, Johnny Unitas's salary of $125,000 would be equivalent to $1 million today, adjusted for inflation. Today, quarterbacks are being paid twenty to thirty times more than he would have made.

Interestingly, 80 percent of the Miami Dolphins games I've attended had a flyover as well as some representatives from the military present or participating in the anthem. I see taking a knee as disrespecting the very flag brave men and women have died defending so these players could have rights and freedoms.

I don't even know what the NFL protests are about anymore. If it's police brutality against African-Americans, as Colin Kaepernick of the 49ers intended, better ways for these millionaires to protest must exist. Why piss off their fan base?

What does the American flag and our national anthem have to do with potentially questionable police tactics? To me, it just seems like follow-the-leader games, with the next guy not fully understanding why he took a knee in the first place.

Another time, one guy stood outside the tunnel for the anthem while all others remained inside. With poor communication and poor organization, the demonstration is losing its meaning for me. Arranging team meetings with local congressmen, politicians, or the heads of the police precincts where such brutality might occur might give more meaning—and better press coverage—to their cause.

I suppose what surprises me most is how I see other citizens treating our flag and national anthem. Perhaps this should be expected when highly paid NFL players are taking a knee in protest, while police personnel and stadium security look on. We have neighbors getting upset and destroying others' property because they are displaying the American flag. High schools are banning American flags on clothing. I recently read where the American flag is not to be worn or displayed in school. It's on the list of items *not allowed at schools.* Think about this for a second. We're in America, yet the flag is banned because it is potentially offensive to others. Yet, I suppose a kid could wear the Iranian flag, Syrian flag, or other more controversial items because they are not specifically listed as banned. Incredible.

We have become a country of sissies, starting with the new breed of educators. We are truly unorganized as a people, my friends, and that's precisely what our enemies want. We will be weaker and have less strength if we are unorganized and broken apart.

This is very confusing to me. Have we abandoned our flag, our anthem, and everything they stand for? Do we remember why we salute our flag and once said the pledge of allegiance every morning in school? Students in our schools now have the right to protest the national anthem and pledge of allegiance. I suppose this wouldn't be as big of an issue to me if the kids were taught the meaning of such things in the first place. If they really understood what "The Star-Spangled Banner" lyrics symbolize and mean, would they be showing such disrespect to our anthem?

While I understand First Amendment rights, I do not believe educators are truly teaching our kids the meaning of the flag and what it stands for in the first place. The respect for our country's flag and everything it stands for is held in the highest regard by our armed forces, police forces, homeland security, and the many government agencies whose sole mission is to protect the citizens of the United States, day in and day out. At this very point in time, a debate rages about police protection or armed guards within our schools. Why, then, would the very kids who would require such protection want to show such disrespect? Teenagers are rebellious in their own right and don't need provocation. Our educators need to do a better job with education and not spinning history as they see fit. We need our kids to be given the vital information so that they are informed and can make such decisions for themselves. By the time these naysayers are done, there will be nothing left for the kids to even challenge. Geez.

The anthem is particularly special to me as Key, attorney and amateur poet, wrote the famous song so close to my hometown. Living so close to Fort McHenry, we took

CHAPTER 11

Democratic Socialism

As we see a new wave of socialist beliefs amongst many Hollywood elites and certain Democrats, I think we can make a comparison to parenting. Kids will often do the exact opposite of what their parents might want them to do. Since President Trump has taken office, the Democrats seem to do the exact opposite of everything he wants. I often wonder, why do so many of Hollywood's elite advocate for democratic socialism when capitalism made them rich? Can these people point to a single nation that has been successful with socialism, whose citizens are not living in squalor?

Socialism is the big lie of the twenty-first century. It promises prosperity, equality, and security. It delivers poverty, misery, and tyranny. In a capitalist economy, incentives are key. The profit-and-loss system of accounting, market prices, and private property rights provide an efficient, interrelated system of incentives to guide and direct economic behavior. Capitalism is based on the theory that incentives matter. Under socialism, incentives either play a minimal role or no role at all. A centrally planned economy without market prices or profits, where property is owned by the state, is a system without an effective incentive mechanism to direct economic activity.

In failing to emphasize incentives, socialism is a theory inconsistent with human nature and is, therefore, doomed to failure. Socialism is based on the premise that incentives don't matter. The main difference between capitalism and socialism is that capitalism works. Now, let's take a quick peek at some socialist countries to better understand the potential flaws:

- China: the government manages and controls the economy
- Denmark: highest taxes in the world
- Ireland: 25 percent of their GDP goes toward paying for their welfare system

Cuba, North Korea, Venezuela, Syria, Libya, Russia, South Yemen, and Algeria are other examples of countries who've embraced socialism.

For the multimillionaire Hollywood elites, like Sean Penn, Michael Moore, Danny Glover, and others who admire socialist policies, why don't they liquidate their resources and distribute these monies equally to those less fortunate? Taking such action would have significantly more meaning to me than taking advantage of their notoriety and using the media and other sources to get their message out.

Because I consider these entertainers bright, educated people, I am surprised they could be so naïve in this regard. These same people stand for illegal immigrants crossing our borders, sanctuary cities, and so forth. Why would those from Mexico, Central America, Syria, Eastern Europe, and other countries flee their countries to come to America in the first place? Is it because of some of the flawed policies in their own countries? Maybe the following example will put this in perspective for you.

Joe Legal works in construction, has a social security number, and makes twenty-five dollars an hour, with taxes deducted.

José Illegal also works in construction, has no social security number, and makes fifteen dollars an hour in cash, under the table.

Ready? Now, pay attention.

Joe Legal, at twenty-five dollars per hour times forty hours, makes $1,000 per week or $52,000 per year. Now, take 31 percent away for state and federal taxes. Joe Legal now has $31,231.

José Illegal gets fifteen dollars per hour times forty hours, which equals $600 per week or $31,200 dollars per year. José Illegal pays no taxes and now has $31,200.

Joe Legal pays medical and dental insurance with limited coverage for his family at $600 per month or $7,200 per year. Joe Legal now has $24,031.

José Illegal has full medical and dental coverage through state and local clinics and emergency hospitals at a cost of zero dollars per year. José Illegal still has $31,200.

Joe Legal makes too much money and is not eligible for food stamps or welfare. Joe Legal spends $500 per month/$6,000 per year for food. Joe Legal now has $18,031.

José Illegal has no documented income and is eligible for food stamps, WIC, and welfare. José Illegal still has $31,200.

Joe Legal pays rent of $1,200 per month/$14,400 per year. Joe Legal now has $9,631.

José Illegal receives $500 per month in federal rent subsidy. José Illegal pays out that $500 per month/$6,000 per year. José Illegal still has $31,200.

Joe Legal pays $200 per month/$2,400 per year for insurance. Some of that is uninsured motorist insurance. Joe Legal now has $7,231.

José Illegal says, "We don't need no stinkin' insurance," and still has $31,200.

José Illegal has to make his $31,200 stretch to pay utilities, gasoline, and what he sends out of the country every month.

Joe Legal now works overtime on Saturdays or gets a part-time job after work.

José Illegal has nights and weekends off to enjoy with his family.

Joe Legal's and José Illegal's children both attend the same elementary school.

Joe Legal pays for his children's lunches, while José Illegal's children get a government-sponsored lunch.

José Illegal's children attend an after-school ESL program.
Joe Legal's children go home.

Now, when they reach college age, Joe Legal's kids may not get into a state school and may not qualify for scholarships, grants, or other tuition help, even though Joe has been paying for state schools through taxes.

José Illegal's kids go to the head of the class because they are a minority.

Joe Legal and José Illegal both benefit from the same police services, but Joe paid for them and José did not.

Do you get it now?

If we vote for or support any politician who supports illegal aliens and democratic socialism, we are part of the problem—not the solution. I've thought about why some of these Hollywood elites and politicians would push for socialism. For politicians, is it just about the votes?

Admittedly, when I was fresh out of high school and had to pay my own way for college and everything else, I was broke. Free stuff would have been enticing. Now that I'm older and wiser, I understand there's no such thing as free stuff. If furniture stores advertise incredible deals, zero interest, and 50 percent off, then shouldn't we be smart enough to know that there is a huge markup in the first place? Nothing in life is free; it's all in how it's presented to the buyer. Free tuition, free healthcare, free this, and free that is very appealing to those who cannot afford such things in the first place. Wouldn't we be better off as a society if healthcare was priced right and people could afford such things?

And, for the same people who despise this president and support illegal immigration, aren't you smart enough to know why these people want to come here in the first place? After all, if our country was like theirs, they would stay home.

CHAPTER 12

The Social Media Generation

I am not a politician out on a book tour, nor do I have a platform by which to support my new book. It seems every public official is on a book or speech tour today, making far more money than when they were in office. If these officials were contemplating writing a book while still in office, were they documenting all their thoughts and meetings, perhaps violating laws in the process? Has the social media generation of text messaging, smartphones, and emails desensitized us to how we are treating others? High-profile public officials on book tours in 2018 alone include James Comey, Hillary Clinton, Bill Clinton, and Omarosa Manigault. Hillary

Clinton signed a book deal with Simon and Schuster in 2001 for $8 million before she became secretary of state. If these books are about your life, you might make life a bit more exciting, as was the case for James Comey. Wouldn't some purposefully do that? Anyway, ponder that point as you read on.

I'll show off my age here. I can recall three specific technologies that made a major impact on how we do business today: the fax machine, Federal Express, and the cell phone. Despite these three technological advancements, they really allowed us to communicate faster, *not differently*. These three tools made us more efficient, primarily in our business lives. I can still recall the days I did not have a cell phone and would pull over to my favorite Holiday Inn on Ulmerton Road in Clearwater, Florida, to utilize their phone bank to make business calls and schedule appointments.

Nobody had a competitive advantage as we were all utilizing the same tools at that time. We used our desk phones to schedule most of our appointments or pay phones with calling cards if we were on the road. We would stuff large envelopes with our product literature and formally mail quotes. For those of us who endured these times, we truly appreciate the advancements of these new technologies and the impact they've had on our business lives. While these tools had a drastic impact on how quickly and effectively we could communicate, they really didn't change what we communicated or how. They were simply more efficient.

Now, we'll fast-forward to the advent of the internet. I am an engineer in a high-technology-based field; however, it still amazes me that this World Wide Web is available to us twenty-four seven. The World Wide Web is at the very heart of everything we do and touch now, every day. I often think about our approach to education when I ponder social media. In schools, children are taught how to read books. They are taught (or *were* taught) how to write and write papers or essays for English class after reading a novel. If we are to prepare kids for this technology-saturated world, doesn't this approach to education seem "old school"? We are taught verbs and adjectives and how to construct sentences for writing; however, no class teaches text messaging or how to construct a proper email.

I'll bet you didn't know that $395 billion in online sales were reported by the United States Department of E-Commerce in 2016. Wow! I'll bet every reader has bought something online this year. Why wouldn't we? We can do product comparisons online and analyze various distributors and prices. We've come to trust online venders as we can read consumer ratings. Access to robust purchasing information means we've become very educated shoppers in this process. No longer do we succumb to pushy sales pitches given by the clerk at the store.

This new purchasing paradigm applies to hotels, airfares, and vacation packages, too. The internet has certainly changed our lives forever and shunned the travel agent in the process. And what about the post office? If it weren't for bulk mail (junk mail), this institution would have closed years ago. Many pay bills online, are going green with various statements, and don't write letters or send cards as we used to.

As with anything, both advantages as well as disadvantages come with our use of technology. Let's take a look at the advantages of shopping online:

- Saves money
- Saves time
- Saves gas

Now, let's take a look at some of the disadvantages:

- Retailers incur high costs to rent space, which provides us the convenience of having the store nearby, and their margins are shrinking; many are going out of business, including Sears, which started their first catalog business in 1889.
- Cookies are small files embedded on your phone, laptop, iPad, or other smart device to track website activity. Didn't you ever wonder why you get emails or pop-ups suggesting, with eerie accuracy, products you might be interested in? (And although I don't like the guy, I do not believe Tom Brady uses sports enhancement drugs, which get advertised to me every so often, to burn fat, pack on muscle, and skyrocket energy.)
- Returns convenience: While one can make returns with products purchased online, the transaction is electronic, with no face-to-face communication. Thus, some vendors simply don't feel that they have to treat the customer with kid gloves. Priceline is a good example. Back in 2004, when Florida was getting pummeled by hurricanes, I booked the Holiday Inn on the beach in Melbourne for two nights for business. This was booked in advance. I couldn't make the trip and leave my family during a hurricane, and the hotel was actually destroyed by the storm. As payments are

guaranteed, Priceline still wanted to charge me for the stay. After several calls, I resolved this, but it was a hassle and more stressful than handling the issue face-to-face. Returns for electronic transactions are "cold" and typically include no direct human interaction.

I use the Web, religiously, every day for research or to confirm facts. However, the younger generation was born into the age of the internet. They know no differently. They don't know about rotary phones, fax machines, or even large hard drives (they keep everything backed up in the cloud). But younger folks must realize others have access to their every online move. The demographics created today are smarter than ever. They capture what we like to eat, where we like to eat, where we shop, where we travel, our favorite hotel brands, and so much more.

This information is invaluable to the vendor. How many times have you shopped a particular vacation spot and then received uninvited emails or pop-ups within web pages specific to the location you were researching? That's just cookie activity. If you link your calendar on your phone using Google or another app, every single entry in your calendar is on the Web.

About a year and a half ago, I was shopping locally for a new laptop at a large retailer. I was semi-interested in the Windows Surface laptops but realized I would be going backwards compared to the options I had on my current laptop. The Surface device had no disk drive, had a two-hundred or three-hundred-gigabyte hard drive, less HDMI inputs, and so forth. When I asked the tech geek at the store about the size of the hard drives on the new laptops, he asked,

"Don't you store stuff in the cloud?" Incredible. That tells me that the younger generations are doing just that.

Why, then, would a company such as Microsoft preconfigure systems with so little storage? Electronic devices, unlike furniture, have a very low profit margin. Stores do not generally keep extra stock of many items. Since everyone has smartphones or iPads, and camera technology in these devices continues to get better and better, video files and picture files are getting larger. Unless you have your own NAS drive at home, large hard drive, or other backup drives, you will run out of storage space quickly. Is this a conscious decision by these suppliers?

Social media has profoundly affected younger generations, just as earlier technologies impacted mine. The difference, however, is that communication has changed. Let's take a look at some examples of how life has changed for our teens and kids.

School: If you have children in school, you are undoubtedly using an online program called SIS Gateway, or something similar, to receive text messages. This program alerts you if your child is tardy or misses a class; you can also see all your child's grades. On the one hand, these new tools seem extremely efficient; on the other, I get the feeling of invasion of privacy. Even so, I give these tools an *A* grade for providing objective information on assignment grades and attendance.

Shopping: Though we've discussed numerous benefits to shopping online, remember, one must be aware of and perhaps guarded against targeted marketing efforts. Periodically, you should unsubscribe to the lists your email address was added to as a result of a sale or applying for a coupon. I give these tools a *B* grade because of their impact on local retailers. How many of us have shopped a product locally, only to buy it online at a significantly reduced price? Trust me. You can work with the hometown retailer as they will all price match. Give them the chance. After all, if they're all gone in the future, we will be screwed, trusting a two-inch picture for a $600 purchase.

Dating: I have been divorced and on my own for five years now, so I have dabbled on dating sites. I know many who have used these sites for hookups, dating, or marriage. Not for me, but I can't deny this large business segment born of the social media age. I simply cannot believe how much information people post about themselves online for everyone to see, including sickos, pervs, predators, and the like. While many good people place profiles on these sites, I fear they are unaware of the sickos who might be stalking them.

A funny, quick story, before my rating. A good friend of mine was bragging about Plenty of Fish (POF), a dating site he was using to get lots of dates and meet some great women. On one occasion, since his date had a profile that said she was a boater, he invited her to his boat for a glass of wine after dinner. The boat was docked in calm waters, but within fifteen to twenty minutes, his date was throwing up over the rails of the boat. You can say or post anything you want on a dating site, and his story somewhat tarnished the image of online dating for me. I would have to give these tools a *C*. I didn't give a worse grade as I really have very little experience and never actually went on an online date. I suppose I'm a bit old-fashioned and still believe that meeting someone through a friend, at the gym, or by sharing a common interest is better than the online stuff.

Friendships: Here, I am including friends you connect with through Facebook, text messaging, Snapchat, instant messaging, Spaces, or other sites. I recall dropping my daughter off at the Boca Town Center Mall to meet her friends one Saturday afternoon. She was sending countless text messages back and forth as I was driving in circles in the parking lot. I finally told her to *call* her girlfriend so we would know where to meet. The impact of text messaging on friendships today cannot be underestimated. I'm a bit old-fashioned and can type more quickly on a laptop, so I actually prefer emails. But text messaging is used today for dating, communication between kids and their parents, communication with teachers, and communication between friends. While these tools have advantages, and some people even find solace in using Facebook as an outlet, I see three fundamental flaws with these technologies:

1. Education: Including the likes of Donald Trump, nobody has received education on how to communicate via tweets, text messaging, Facebook, etc. Everything is subject to interpretation by the other party; tone of voice and body language is lost. You also might say things in a text or on Facebook you'd never say directly to a person.

2. Interpersonal skills: People skills are lost among this generation. If greater than 90 percent of communications are done electronically, the conversation is one-sided and drastically different than in-person dialogue. Text messages and emails are a cop-out for hard, face-to-face discussions. Electronic communication is also a bit plastic and phony to me.

If my observations are valid, then people are getting a false sense of security through this type of messaging.

3. Real friends: it seems that many people are more concerned with the sheer number of friends they might have on Facebook. Doesn't this create a false sense or feeling of security? When I was a kid, it seemed that we could count our real friends on one hand. I have friends on Facebook that have well over a thousand friends. Really? And then people go on to share their most intimate thoughts or actions with people that they don't even really know! What are the longer-term impacts of this false sense of security with these virtual friendships?

Therefore, I give social tools a *D*. Like eating ice cream or drinking wine, everything is fine in moderation. I believe that we'd all benefit from limiting the amount of time spent on text-messaging and Facebook. Statistics show that the average person spends 135 minutes per day on social media. If a person sleeps eight hours per day, this equates to 13 percent of their waking hours.

News: I have a quick story to share here that puts all the fake news into perspective. My sixteen-year-old son loves rap and hip-hop music. I support this, within reason; after all, my dad hated my music when I was a teenager as well. I listened to hair bands and hard rock bands like Judas Priest and Van Halen. My mom and dad supported me in buying those albums and playing the music.

In 2017, I decided to take Christopher to a Snoop Dogg concert as he enjoys rap music, even though I do not. Christopher knows I have a lot of passion for NFL football and the Miami Dolphins, so he says to me, "Dad, did you know that Snoop Dogg played in the NFL?" Stop right there! Of course, I had to search Google to see why my son might believe this skinny rapper played in the NFL.

When you google Snoop Dogg and NFL, you see a link to his appearance on *The Ellen DeGeneres Show*; the caption reads that he once coached Pittsburgh Steelers's JuJu Smith-Schuster, a wide receiver, and Kansas City Chiefs's De'Anthony Thomas, a return specialist and defensive end. If you google JuJu Smith-Schuster, you'll see absolutely no reference to Snoop Dogg. However, Snoop Dog was a coach and had his Youth Football League (SYFL) in Los Angeles. The league is focused on inner-city kids, aged between five and thirteen. Snoop Dogg never played for the NFL, but he did, in fact, coach several kids who went on to play in the NFL.

When we read a newspaper or watched the news in the 60s, even into the 80s, we believed every word we read or heard. The problem today is that news is released very quickly on the internet. Stories are not researched nor facts validated, but many people take this information at face value and run with it. This rush-to-publication form of media is having a direct impact on how people think and behave. It's quite dangerous if the facts are inaccurate.

The Russians have always been a very sophisticated and intelligent people. Why, then, have they infiltrated Facebook and other news sources to spread propaganda and potentially impact how voters think? Back to the Snoop Dogg story to make a point here. My son knows Dad hates rap and loves the NFL. He took limited information that was either prespun, or spun out of control on its own, to persuade me to respect this rapper. This was the tactic of a sixteen-year-old boy.

Imagine the tactics of the KGB or foreign government or other news media outlets. I would have to give these tools an *F*. While I believe internet news sources have the potential for great value, it seems media giants like Google, Facebook, Twitter, and others are torn between our First Amendment rights and verifiable information and sources. Nonetheless, these industry giants have control over a majority of people today. This would imply that we "get what we get and don't get upset."

In short, we are all a part of the social media generation and use these tools every day. We need to be prudent, however, in our use of such information. Does our research go deep enough? Do we analyze multiple stories about the same subject? Do we draw our own conclusions on misinformation? Undoubtedly, every age group has become reliant on these tools and trusts them every day. Whether doing our online banking, getting decorating ideas, comparing auto prices, booking a hotel, or finding reasons to hate the sitting president, we would be lost without such tools.

Maybe I'm just a little suspicious about the likes of Amazon, Google, and some of the products being brought to market and their intention. Let's look at the Roomba robotic vacuum system from iRobot, for example. Certain models of this unit will tie right into your Wi-Fi connection if you allow it. Why? As this robot follows a mapping sequence in a room or particular floor, does it collect data? Does it know that you could use a piece of furniture in the corner of a particular room? Will that data be shared with vendors? I don't know about you, but I receive confidential information documents almost weekly about what data is being shared, and you have the ability to opt out. Does this mean that every time we

CHAPTER 13

The Silent Majority

I t has long been my contention that the people who elected Donald Trump were a silent majority. This large community can be broken down into several groups: veterans, those serving in the armed services, or as police and border security agents; small-business men and women; blue-collar workers; the forgotten man (Hillary might have referred to this group of people as the "deplorables"); people who feel the government let them down; free marketeers (free traders in favor of smaller government, with moderate to liberal views on immigration); American preservationists; staunch conservatives or loyal Republicans; and anti-elites (those who believe economic and political systems are rigged). Quiet still today, this silent majority listens, watches, and observes how this president behaves, the policies he implements, and how the media attacks him every step of the way.

The silent majority didn't put the signs on their lawns or bumper stickers on their cars; they didn't start bar fights over political beliefs. This group of believers was silent in their opinions and views but had a strong alignment with what then-candidate Trump believed in. They were hoping and praying for a better tomorrow and humble in their approach to this past presidential election.

Interestingly, a majority of people who supported and voted for Donald J. Trump didn't care for his style or persona. Maybe this is why so many were *silent* in the first place. Even the pollsters, for the most part, got it wrong and didn't see his win coming. But aligning with the perhaps obnoxious behavior of President Trump has nothing to do with aligning with his values, his principles, and his overall ambition to "Make America Great Again."

His motto struck a chord with at least half of the country. I believe a large group of voters did not like candidate Trump, even if they believed in what he stood for, so they voted for Hillary or didn't vote at all. Think about this. Midwestern people from the smaller suburbs in America, blue-collar, hardworking Americans—who couldn't be more different than a loud and boisterous New Yorker—identified with his values, campaign promises, and overall message about our great country.

I suppose the lesson for historians, reporters, and all the experts who follow presidential elections is to never, ever underestimate the silent majority. Just because some people don't scream at the top of their lungs in inner cities as they walk past the poor homeless people living on the streets, doesn't mean that the homeless people aren't there and that they don't care. Just because someone doesn't show up at city hall to argue with city officials over policy doesn't mean he doesn't care. Just because someone doesn't take a position in a restaurant, bus, or bar when a political debate is going on doesn't mean they don't care or have an opinion. Just because Johnny at work hasn't really said anything about the election process or candidates doesn't mean he doesn't have thoughts on both.

The experts really got it wrong during this last election cycle, and hopefully a lesson was learned. Despite the easy, unceasing exchange of ideas made possible by social media, a good majority of people were rather silent in how they approached the election and the months beyond. These people were not chanting in the streets, confronting the opposition, or threatening to blow up the White House. No, this is the silent majority, and they are still there.

So, while the protests continue, along with president bashing, media outrage, and negative commentaries, what is going on with this silent majority? Is it being dismantled? Is it shrinking? I don't think so. I believe this very large group of people are so disgusted by the constant attacks in the media and amongst various politicians and actual bullies that they will defend and support the person being so viciously attacked. I'm not certain this group of initial supporters will grow, but I do not think it will be intimidated or shrink. Only time will tell the story. We will know more in the next presidential election cycle for sure.

Since the silent majority is just that—silent—this is a hard group to read when it comes to demographics. They are not loud, boisterous, or otherwise causing a stir, and they might not even participate in polls. These people are going about their lives, whether protecting our border, building a car, preventing a burglary, or getting their children ready for a day at school. They probably watch the news but may never share their feelings about what they read or heard with anyone at work, with their neighbors, or perhaps even their loved ones. Just as it is hard to understand or get inside the mind of a hater, so, too, is it hard to identify the silent majority.

I've never quite understood undecided voters. I imagine they are not hardcore Democrats or Republicans, and perhaps they do not vote straight down party line in every election cycle. It's rather hard for me to identify with them. After so many debates during an election cycle and all the available information on various candidates, how can these voters still be undecided? The fact is, this segment represented 13-20 percent of voters in past elections. This invisible, undecided voter or "swing voter" might be considered the silent *minority*. That being said, and not having a clue when it comes to the news media and facts that they rely on when putting together their news stories, why in the h*** wouldn't the media consider this large group of Americans when putting together their stories?

I've often reflected on my own business and personal experiences when covering these topics, so I cannot help but share a story here. A company's decision to buy capital equipment, which can cost hundreds of thousands of dollars to the end user, could actually threaten job security. While I meet with engineers working on a particular project, and oftentimes their management, I do not always get to meet the top brass and executives who ultimately support or deny a decision to buy. Although a silent minority, this exists in my own personal business and I deal with it on a daily basis. Sales don't rest on what is being said and shared at meetings; I also need to know my customer's unspoken needs; I must listen to what they want, but deliver what they need. My company must anticipate the needs of upper management.

Donald J. Trump did just that during this past election cycle. He knew how to read his audience and anticipated their needs. The silent majority has been quiet for decades after all. They never shouted, "Build that wall," but they supported the idea. They never said, "Death to all terrorists and those who would attack America," but they supported policies to destroy ISIS. They never shouted, "I'm sick and disgusted with decades of outsourcing our technology and manufacturing jobs to China and offshore," but they supported bringing jobs back to our country. As this past election was the largest upset in American presidential history, I have to give it to Trump for having the courage to anticipate the needs of the people and convey a message that resonated with the American voter. Quite an accomplishment, for sure.

A significant part of this silent majority are those brave men and women who fought in wars and carried out their missions so many miles away to keep us safe right here at home. After retiring or completing their mission, they don't typically wear uniforms in public or rant about all they endured on our behalf. These veterans are amongst us as we go on our merry way in life. To say these brave men and women put their lives on the line to protect those who now ridicule their efforts and what they have done is an understatement.

I'm reminded of a story from an acquaintance about a small group of marines, the 2d ANGLICO Marines in Somalia, the history of which dates back to the original formation of Joint Assault Signals Company (JASCO) units who fought in World War II. These units were used to coordinate air, artillery, and naval gunfire support between the Marines, Army, and US Navy. It was in 1949 that the Marine Corps began the process of recreating the JASCO capability under the new ANGLICO designation. ANGLICO, 2d signals battalion, 2d marine divisions was formed in December, 1949 at Camp Lejeune, North Carolina.

My acquaintance, a marine sergeant, shared his story about what he saw and endured with his battalion in Somalia in 1992. As tears came to this grown man's eyes, he shared how this strong and elite group of fighters were given orders to go through villages where American soldiers were despised, where they encountered mass starvation and people dying. We don't seem to relate to the experiences of the countless heroes in America who are part of this silent majority. While typically proud of all they have accomplished on behalf of Americans, they are also modest, despite what they have endured along the way.

So, to the thousands of pollsters, newscasters, and otherwise experts who seem to have all the answers, I say, never underestimate the silent majority. Try to identify with this particular audience if you can, or it'll be another "gotcha" moment!

CHAPTER 14

Political Incorrectness

This chapter is deserving of a book all its own, for sure. Political incorrectness is the attitude displayed by those who do not care if they offend or upset another group in society who is at a disadvantage or who has been treated differently because of their sex, race, or disability.

I recall an incident about four years ago when I was walking with my son in downtown Boca Raton. I turned to him and said, "You know, buddy, when you get your basketball trophy tomorrow, you'll have way more trophies than your dad ever got." At just eleven years old, he looked up at me and said, "Your dad didn't get you involved in sports like you do with me?" I retorted, "H***, yeah. Except when your dad was in sports, we only got a trophy if we came in first, maybe second place!"

It's both incredible and frustrating to witness the antics that go on daily regarding "political correctness." From the Boy Scouts of America changing their name to the Scouts of America, to coed bathrooms, to the "everyone gets a trophy generation," to sanctuary cities and so much more, we have become a country of sissies. For every action, there is a reaction. For example, as we teach our kids they are all winners—no losers—we have taken away one of the most important learning experiences of their formative years: failure. Failures make us stronger as we learn from our mistakes. Without mistakes, how are we to learn? How can we try harder next time? Run faster? Go from a B in a class to an A?

I cannot be the only person questioning just what the heck is going on with our country, our values, and our wonderful American people. Review the list below and truly try to find any benefit, whatsoever:

- May 2, 2018: After a 108-year history as the Boy Scouts of America, the organization changed its name to Scouts BSA. We have the Girl Scouts of America as well, and I continue to scratch my head when decisions like this are made to appease a very small minority, allowing girls to join what was once the Boy Scouts of America. I must have missed that meeting.
- May 8, 2018: Hanover Park High School in East Hanover, New Jersey, says the cheerleading team must accept everyone or be disbanded. Once again, everyone gets a trophy no matter what. What about

the girls who have worked hard for years to make that team? What do these policies say to them, that working hard doesn't pay off?

- Various high schools have banned the wearing of American flags in an effort to be inclusive. If Italian-Americans, Puerto Ricans, Mexican immigrants, or others are proud of their heritage and allowed to display their flags on their clothing, automobiles, etc., why shouldn't Americans born in this country be given that same privilege?

- July 21, 2018: Hillary Clinton wants to offer free flight tickets to illegals to reunite families.

- June 2018: Far-left Democrats have a rallying cry to "Abolish ICE," our Immigration and Customs Enforcement agency. Are the politicians calling for this really willing to compromise our public safety?

- Sanctuary Cities across America: The very definition of a sanctuary city states that it "limits their cooperation with the national government's effort to enforce immigration laws." The leaders of these cities want to reduce the fear of deportation and possible family breakup among people who are in our country illegally. More than five hundred US jurisdictions, including states and municipalities, have adopted sanctuary policies. So, if I understand the reasoning correctly, these policies are being put into place because we have people who are already here illegally and don't want to get caught.

- Organizations are calling on people to incite violence and protests. Steve Scalise, a Republican in the House of Representatives, was shot at a ballpark when the shooter opened fire on GOP members of Congress. Pam Bundy, Republican attorney general for Florida, and her boyfriend were harassed at a movie theater in Tallahassee, Florida. Sarah Huckabee Sanders and her family were refused dinner at the Red Hen restaurant in Lexington, Virginia, because she works for Donald Trump.

If we apply the definition of political incorrectness in each one of these instances, we can find where these policies are offending people in society who have a disadvantage. The disadvantage is that the system truly does appear to be "rigged" in every way. Let's take a quick look at those who might be affected by these policies.

Boy Scouts of America has been around for 108 years for boys ages eleven to seventeen. What about those who might have been in Cub Scouts prior to joining the Boy Scouts of America? For their younger years, they were dreaming of the days that they would become a proud Boy Scout in the Boy Scouts of America. What do they think of this new name? Are they offended? Are they at a distinct disadvantage that they had absolutely no say over this name change?

The same goes for those cheerleaders who worked hard for so many years to make that squad at the high school in New Jersey. One mother starts whining because her daughter didn't make the team, and now they must allow anyone to be a cheerleader? Is there a distinct disadvantage here to the girls who already made the team? Is this reverse discrimination? Just how many cheerleaders can be on a squad anyway? The disadvantage in this particular case might be that the cheerleaders' moms were rather quiet when their daughters made the team. They didn't cause an uproar or a stir. Incredible situations, folks.

If my son tried out for the high school football team and didn't make the team because other kids were faster, stronger, or overall better athletes, I would hardly expect the rules to be changed to simply accommodate my son. Are these policies fair? Remember, everyone is created equal, but that's only the start. If someone studies harder and is more dedicated with their homework, she will more likely get better grades. What's next? Everyone will get an *A* just for showing up?

And what about the protests where violence is being incited by various groups and individuals? Are the people that might show up for a protest to defend a different position at a distinct disadvantage as they planned to attend such an event in a peaceful and meaningful manner? People being pelted with rocks, people enraged looking to drive fear into people that have a difference of opinion.

I'm a strong advocate for looking back at history and seeing what it teaches. Whether a business decision or a decision I made while on the board of directors for my HOA, I would never support a decision that did not have broad support. The problem in today's society is that the crybabies and naysayers are the ones showing up at various town hall meetings and getting their points across. Although they might represent .00001 percent of the school or district, they show up, have built a case, and present it to people who lack the experience in making such decisions.

It just seems to me that anyone behind any of the policy decisions discussed above never followed the old phrase, "If it ain't broke, don't fix it." While it might seem that this phrase has been around forever and comes from the Roosevelt or

Truman era, it's only been around since 1977. T. Bert (Thomas Bertram) Lance was the director of the office of management and budget in Jimmy Carter's administration. Imagine that, a Democrat. Where are these guys hiding nowadays? The story behind his motto was that he believed he could save the US Government billions of dollars if he could get them to adopt this premise. He went on to explain in a newsletter in the US Chamber of Commerce, *Nation's Business*, May 1977: "If it ain't broke, don't fix it. That's the trouble with government: fixing things that aren't broken and not fixing things broken."

Interesting food for thought, for sure, and I had no idea of the origin of this motto I had been using for years. I'm wondering if our compassion has been lost with these new ideals and what we often refer to as political correctness. Do the politicians supporting these ideals truly do the checks and balances to see what percentage of Americans might benefit and what percentage will be hurt by these policies? I simply cannot believe the people behind these new programs and ideas are mean or vindictive; perhaps they are just naïve. It seems one who would devote his career to being a politician would likely feel compassionate toward the American people—*all Americans*, not a select few. Don't be a hypocrite and discriminate. Don't attack the rich for being rich and successful. Don't attack the *Boy* Scouts of America and don't attack our hard-working cheerleaders who practice every day. Rewards should be earned, not given. How about getting back to some good, old-fashioned common sense, okay?

It seems to me that the "silent majority" is much too passive today, hence such politically incorrect decisions are being made. Why are we allowing major policy decisions to be made and changed for the people who simply show up? A good analogy here is Yelp and ratings for various restaurants. I *never* trust these. Do those who enjoyed a great meal usually take the time to discuss that? Or is it the whiner who has something bad to say about every restaurant who takes the time to do this?

CHAPTER 15

Constantly under Attack

P resident Trump is in the crosshairs with the media and many citizens almost daily. This makes for a very tough situation for his public relations people and those closest to him in his cabinet. Donald J. Trump has an alter ego whereby he has thrived in front of cameras for most of his adult career. He hails from Queens, New York, has built some of the most luxurious properties and hotels in the world, started an airline that bore his name, and is basically a show-off. I can't help but compare Trump to other show-offs and multibillionaires, like George Steinbrenner, Jerry Jones, Al Davis, George Soros, and Elon Musk.

On one hand, the media is quite unfair to our current president; a recent study shows coverage is 91 percent negative. Yet, on the other, this president feeds the media and plays them like puppets. The media is at this president's beck and call. While the coverage might be 91 percent negative, his approval rating is actually on par with President Barack Obama during the same time in office. Donald Trump has a history with television shows dating back to the late 80s with *WrestleMania IV* and *V* and then *The Apprentice* from 2003 to 2015. From 1996 to 2015, he was the major owner of the Miss Universe pageant. He thrives on the limelight and is not shy when it comes to media attention. It's the negative attention and publicity, however, that he is not accustomed to.

I'm not certain whether it is Donald Trump, the president and person, or Donald Trump, the personality, under such vicious attack. The media has attacked his children and his wife as well. I always thought personal attack was completely off-limits for any sitting president. Did Chelsea Clinton, the Obama girls, or Michelle Obama receive such scrutiny and ridicule?

In the most recent Gallup poll on June 17, 2018, the president's approval rating is at 45 percent (88 percent amongst Republicans). The gross domestic product growth is at 4.1 percent in the second quarter of the year (highest in four years), unemployment rate of 3.9 percent[4] (an eighteen-year low), North Korea back on their heels, numerous bilateral trade deals in the works, ISIS all but obliterated, a tax reform package that helps all businesses and workers, hundreds of thousands of new manufacturing jobs coming back to

---

4   *Forbes*

America,[5] the steel industry coming back to America, and the world's largest electronics manufacturer opening a plant in Wisconsin (Foxconn, Apple's main manufacturer) where they plan to hire thirteen thousand employees, how and why would this president come under such scrutiny and attack?[6]

The media or "fake news," Trump's popular phrase, simply doesn't get it. They will not win against this president. They called the election in Hillary's favor and lost. The more they attack him, the better his numbers in the polls. We consistently hear it is the swing voters or independents who will determine winners in elections. Why, then, if you are attempting to reach those undecided voters, would you resort to such low tactics, which may alienate that base of voters? Aren't these educated reporters and commentators smarter than that?

I believe I am speaking on behalf of the silent majority when I say, don't play Trump's game; you are certain to lose. He has the experience, he knows how to fight a fight, and when we try to predict his next move, we are often wrong. Just let Trump be Trump. He will not change anytime soon.

I may have lived in South Florida most of my life now, but I still hail from that small suburb outside Baltimore, and most of my traits reflect where I was raised. This is no different for "The Donald." A New Yorker, a mover and a shaker, and a multibillionaire to boot, he is not from Iowa or the Midwest. Trust me, I've lived in Boca Raton since 1984 and am probably part New Yorker myself by now. Love 'em or hate 'em, New Yorkers are a very aggressive people who know exactly what they want and tell it like it is—with no room to second-guess their intent.

5   CNBC
6   All other statistics in this section were derived from the US Bureau of Labor Statistics.

Trump is as transparent as anyone could want a president to be, often tweeting eleven to twelve times per day. Who has done this in the past? The answer, quite simply, is no one. President Trump doesn't go through his PR team or inner circle before sending off these fresh tweets. This guy has empowered the media and gives them fresh stories every day. CNN's ratings are actually at a five-year high. Considering that greater than 90 percent of their coverage is about the president, CNN seemingly needs to thank the president for this ratings boost.

Because this president was a TV reality star, he might have trouble letting go of that persona. Regardless, he's the most powerful man in the world, in charge of the most powerful country in the world. Why would these hate-filled reporters not show respect for the office of the president of the United States? Just as the history books will look back on this presidency to determine the effect this president had on the whole of the United States, they will also look at the media outlets that covered this president, reporting the stories and overall rants.

I am a staunch believer in fair and balanced news. There is no doubt in my mind that Fox News loves Donald Trump as much as CNN hates Donald Trump. Why must it be this way? I know why: it's simply a business. If half the country voted for someone and half voted against someone, either way, it's safe to bet you'll have half the population watching your news networks. Each news outlet feeds its audience what the audience wants to hear. Rosie O'Donnell referred to Fox News on August 7, 2018 as "state-run TV," just like they have in Russia. It's not hard to figure out what news feed she follows.

It's important to learn from our mistakes. We must analyze history when making decisions about the future. If the adage, "Starve a fever, feed a cold," has been proven, why would we attempt different remedies? History has proven what works. Same goes for these vicious attacks against the president of the United States. While these reporters might feed each other during their vicious attack sessions, they are naïve when it comes to the silent majority. After all, that's who got Donald Trump elected in the first place.

Although the president is under daily attacks from the media outlets, he is still our president, as this picture testifies.

CHAPTER 16

Would Dad Have Voted for Trump?

My father died of colon cancer on June 15, 1991. Taken from his wife of thirty-four years and four children at the early age of sixty-four, he left life way too soon. I think of Dad very often and the things I would have loved to have shared with him. We had very deep discussions about all kinds of topics. My dad loved football, especially his Baltimore Colts and the Fighting Irish of Notre Dame. He was a very outspoken man, and you never really had to guess at what he was thinking. He would simply tell you.

He was often the life of the party, and if he went into the grocery store for two items, it would take him an hour because he would talk with everyone in the store. Knowing you or not was inconsequential; he didn't need to warm up to someone to speak plainly. He was a very charming man, with whom people would immediately feel comfortable—even with his rants. Being that Dad was a steelworker and from a lower-middle-class, blue-collar area, he was always a die-hard Democrat. He was a member of the Steelworkers Union and worked at the Sparrows Point steel mill for over forty years as a crane operator in the tin mill. In my childhood neighborhood, Dad was known as "The Mayor of Charlesmont." He was in the middle of everything.

In 1984 while working for Marconi Instruments, I was on a business trip to New Jersey that happened to coincide with Thanksgiving, so I planned to visit my family in Baltimore for that holiday. At the time, two engineers from the factory in Scotland were living in New Jersey. I asked the engineers if they understood the history of our Thanksgiving holiday and the associated traditions. Realizing they were unaware, I explained the history of preparing the feast, watching American football, falling asleep on the couch, and then eating all over again. They were game for experiencing it, so I called my mom to see if I could bring them to Baltimore that holiday weekend, and she was welcoming of our guests.

They showed up at my parents' home bearing gifts of flowers for my mom, candies for my sister, and a bottle of wine for my dad. We were on the porch and not even in the house, yet my dad looked at these guys and said, "I thought your people were cheap." I was absolutely horrified. I had brought two business associates to my parents' home to enjoy Thanksgiving, and my dad just humiliated me. We got settled in the house, and I pulled one of the guys aside and said, "I am so sorry for my dad's comments." Allan looked at me and said, "Oh, you didn't know? We Scots do have a reputation for being very frugal." I had no idea. Dad just told it like it was, no matter who you were.

A lot has changed in our country in the twenty-seven years Dad has been gone. I often think of him and what he, a veteran of the Korean War, might say about certain current events, like NFL players protesting our national anthem, various wars, the situation in North Korea, and much more. So many unanswered questions as he left us so long ago. He never had the opportunity to meet my children, his grandchildren. I'll never know what they would have thought of him.

In trying to determine whether my dad would have voted for Donald Trump, I've considered the following points:

- Trump is "loud and sassy," and although my dad had a lot of those same tendencies, I'm not sure what he would have thought of the president's demeanor.
- Trump wants to fix things he considers to be broken in our country, and I believe Dad would agree that things need to change.
- Trump is touting more American jobs and fewer regulations; he wants to bring steel manufacturing back to America. Dad would be a strong supporter of these policies.
- Trump's support of the veterans, as well as his slogan "Make America Great Again," would rouse support

from my dad. My father was proud to be a veteran and often went to the VFW for meals and social events. According to his wishes, Dad's casket was covered with an American flag.

The more I think about it, the more I believe my father would have voted for Donald J. Trump. He would have approved of his outspokenness, his toughness, his strong support for the military and our police, and his strong national defense policies. Since my dad's own parents came through the system the legal way, he would have also supported Trump's position on illegal immigration.

CHAPTER 17

Inside the Mind of a Hater

In 2008, President Barack Obama, America's first black president, held up *change* as a beacon. He attached this concept to a word that channeled everything his young and diverse coalition saw in his rise and newfound political power: *hope*. Hope was embodied in an America that would elect a black man as president and dare to reach for a future that was different than our past. Just eight years later, Donald J. Trump saw these changes as a threat to the very core of our democracy. He was the voice of many Americans who wanted to make America the way it was before, to make it great *again*.

So, how is it that a country under attack by jihadist extremists of a particular faith could be comprised of political parties with completely different views? On one hand, we had a president for eight years who refused to call ISIS "Islamic terrorists" or acknowledge that enemy and where they were coming from. On the other hand, we have a new president who is banning people from certain countries—referred to as a "Muslim ban" in the media and the left. Our immigration system is broken: gang members arrive from other countries; drugs are smuggled in as we face the worst drug epidemic in our history; the foreign pilots who took down our World Trade Centers were trained in our country. Yet, one side of our country appears not to want to fix our broken immigration laws. They would rather distract the American public, claiming babies are separated from their mothers at the border and children are being held in cages.

I am not privy to the social circles our current politicians, CIA, and DOJ personnel inhabit, so I took a sample of folks around me. While we can see the likes of Lisa Page, Peter Strzok, James Comey, John Brennan, and Michael Moore and consider their comments from afar, I thought it would be helpful to interview fellow citizens for a close-up account of how people on the street feel about President Donald J. Trump.

While American citizens have the right to feel as they choose, it's a matter of national security when we have insiders leaking information, some of which might be classified. It's concerning what some politicians and Washington insiders might do or say to get this president removed from office. If their hatred is so deep for the leader of our country, what risks might they take that could make us vulnerable to our enemies?

Consider Deputy Attorney General Rod Rosenstein. Rosenstein assumed oversight of the DOJ's investigation into Russian election interference after then-Attorney General Jeff Sessions recused himself in 2017. News sources state that Mr. Rosenstein secretly recorded the president in the spring of 2017 and suggested the Twenty-fifth Amendment to remove the president from office for being unfit. Let me ask this, if someone despises Walmart and would never, ever shop there, why in the heck would he want to work there? The same goes for the inner circle and top brass who work for this president—why work there if you despise him so? Is everyone there to gather material to write a book? Is Trump that entertaining?

The American public—as well as presidential aids, cabinet members, and advisors—all deserve their opinions of this president. However, the people in his deep inner circle should not take steps that would detrimentally impact national security. Is it because we are so deeply divided as a people that those closest to this president might feel it's okay to takes such steps?

To promote understanding, I developed a questionnaire and interviewed friends and new acquaintances who are certainly not Trump supporters. Before I began this questionnaire, I asked the interviewees the following questions: Do you hate the president Donald Trump, the person Donald Trump, or the personality of Donald Trump? Unanimously, everyone I polled hated "all of it." Because therapists in the United States are treating patients with what they refer to as "Trump Anxiety Disorder," I saw this was a compelling subject to research.

Interview 1: Allison Delanotte
1. Age? 58
2. Sex? Female
3. Where were you born? Cincinnati, Ohio
4. Where do you live now? Delray Beach, Florida
5. What is your profession? Hostess
6. Did you read Donald Trump's 1987 book, *The Art of the Deal*? No
7. Did you hate Donald Trump before he was elected president—in other words, on day one of his presidency? Yes
8. Do you understand and support sanctuary cities? If yes, why? Don't know what they are.
9. Do you believe the economy is better and stronger today than it was two years ago? No, the prices of food, gas, and other items have gone up.
10. What opinion do you have of loud, obnoxious New Yorkers? Nasty; stay north; annoying in public and on the roadways; pushy in restaurants
11. Do you believe it was a mistake for Hillary Clinton to use a private email server for intragovernment correspondence while she was secretary of state and that information could have ended up in the wrong hands? Yes
12. Do you believe Donald Trump is responsible for the current economy, GDP, and low unemployment rate? Unsure
13. Do you credit Donald Trump and his administration with the decimation of ISIS and the reduction of terror threats in America today? Unsure

14. Do you believe Donald Trump has created the "great divide" in Washington politics today, or was it like that many years prior? Yes, he is the problem.
15. Do you believe our country and culture are facing numerous issues today? Yes
16. Do you believe "incremental change" or "drastic measures" are required to get things back on track? Yes; we need to take baby steps.
17. Do you dislike people who voted for or support Donald Trump? No, but I question the reasons why they voted for him.

Allowed rant: "He is arrogant, a cheater, and offends minorities. He says things hastily. He thinks he's above a lot of people. He can't relate to me. There are so many people in the USA who are struggling just to survive on a daily basis, and he will never be on that level, so he will never be able to relate to or understand what it feels like."

Interview 2: Michelle Keyster
1. Age? 58
2. Sex? Female
3. Where were you born? Baltimore, Maryland
4. Where do you live now? Big Pine Key, Florida
5. What is your profession? Accounting; degree in financial management
6. Did you read Donald Trump's 1987 book, *The Art of the Deal*? No
7. Did you hate Donald Trump before he was elected president—in other words, on day one of his presidency? Yes

8. Do you understand and support sanctuary cities? If yes, why? No, I don't fully understand the topic.

9. Do you believe the economy is better and stronger today than it was two years ago? No; Obama had long-term plans, and Trump eliminated those.

10. What opinion do you have of loud, obnoxious New Yorkers? They're okay; I really don't have a lot of experience with them.

11. Do you believe it was a mistake for Hillary Clinton to use a private email server for intragovernment correspondence while she was secretary of state and that information could have ended up in the wrong hands? Yes

12. Do you believe Donald Trump is responsible for the current economy, GDP, and low unemployment rate? No

13. Do you credit Donald Trump and his administration for the decimation of ISIS and the reduction of terror threats in America today? Unsure. I don't know if we are aware of how many terror attacks might have been thwarted.

14. Do you believe Donald Trump has created the "great divide" in Washington politics today, or was it like that many years prior? I believe this was more hidden before and is permanent now.

15. Do you believe our country and culture are facing numerous issues today? Yes

16. Do you believe "incremental change" or "drastic measures" are required to get things back on track? Yes

17. Do you dislike people who voted for or support Donald Trump? No, people feel slighted.

Allowed rant: "Donald Trump has a history of being a flaming a******, a selfish man, and he has ruined people's lives and never looked back. It pisses me off that our country is divided from the onset as to whether you are a Republican or a Democrat. By separating people and putting them into buckets, we are immediately creating division and causing issues. Donald Trump doesn't show a human side as have the presidents before him. Nobody has done a good job with immigration. Regarding the NFL kneeling and protests there, I have a lot of friends ex-military, and most of them feel that when they signed on the dotted line, they signed for the right for these protests today."

Interview 3: Steth Shenanigans
1. Age: 71
2. Sex: Male
3. Where were you born? Pottersville, Pennsylvania
4. Where do you live now? Islamorada Key, Florida
5. What is your profession? Retired military lieutenant, Vietnam, journalist
6. Did you read Donald Trump's 1987 book, *The Art of the Deal*? No
7. Did you hate Donald Trump before he was elected president—in other words, on day one of his presidency? No, I despise him now, though.
8. Do you understand and support sanctuary cities? If yes, why? Understand, but don't support
9. Do you believe the economy is better and stronger today than it was two years ago? Yes, the stock market is better, if that is the only barometer that you look at.

10. What opinion do you have of loud, obnoxious New Yorkers? They're okay; I used to live in Manhattan; Donald Trump is a narcissist and willfully ignorant.

11. Do you believe it was a mistake for Hillary Clinton to use a private email server for intragovernment correspondence while she was secretary of state and that information could have ended up in the wrong hands? Yes

12. Do you believe Donald Trump is responsible for the current economy, GDP, and low unemployment rate? Uncertain, but this economy is heading for a big fall.

13. Do you credit Donald Trump and his administration for the decimation of ISIS and the reduction of terror threats in America today? No. He is willfully ignorant with such issues like the Iran deal.

14. Do you believe Donald Trump has created the "great divide" in Washington politics today, or was it like that many years prior? I believe there was a crack before, and he's made it into a Grand Canyon.

15. Do you believe our country and culture are facing numerous issues today? Yes

16. Do you believe "incremental change" or "drastic measures" are required to get things back on track? Incremental

17. Do you dislike people who voted for or support Donald Trump? Not necessarily; as a group, yes; individually, no

Allowed rant: "I believe your line of questions showed some bias. You never covered immigration, national security. Not sure where we're headed with this guy, but it doesn't look good. He's a narcissist. His character is in question. He's a liar, a sociopath, and wants to be a dictator."

Interview 4: Dotty Renzonotte

1. Age? 67
2. Sex? Female
3. Where were you born? Brooklyn, New York
4. Where do you live now? Boca Raton, Florida
5. What is your profession? Retired, director, special education
6. Did you read Donald Trump's 1987 book, *The Art of the Deal*? No
7. Did you hate Donald Trump before he was elected president—in other words, on day one of his presidency? No, I hated his personality, though.
8. Do you understand and support sanctuary cities? If yes, why? Yes; our country should embrace everyone and offer protection for them.
9. Do you believe the economy is better and stronger today than it was two years ago? Yes, but I don't attribute this to Donald Trump.
10. What opinion do you have of loud, obnoxious New Yorkers? I'm from New York, and in Florida, you see the worst of the worst.
11. Do you believe it was a mistake for Hillary Clinton to use a private email server for intragovernment correspondence while she was secretary of state and that information could have ended up in the wrong hands? Yes
12. Do you believe Donald Trump is responsible for the current economy, GDP, and low unemployment

rate? Absolutely not. All data shows that it was on an upward curve since the Obama days.

13. Do you credit Donald Trump and his administration for the decimation of ISIS and the reduction of terror threats in America today? No. It was Obama that had Osama bin Laden killed.

14. Do you believe that Donald Trump has created the "great divide" in Washington politics today, or was it like that many years prior? Always been a divide but not like it is today.

15. Do you believe that our country and culture are facing numerous issues today? Yes

16. Do you believe "incremental change" or "drastic measures" are required to get things back on track? Republicans are too afraid to take a stand.

17. Do you dislike people who voted for or support Donald Trump? No, but I lost a lot of respect for some of these people, including family members and friends.

Allowed rant: "Donald Trump has brought about racism. He's a compulsive liar, has no integrity, and will never be my president. It's apparent he's been a money launderer forever; he shows no empathy and will run our deficit into the trillions more. Donald Trump will do whatever it takes to make himself look good. I cannot stand him."

Interview 5: Dotty, the wife

1. Age: 64
2. Sex: Female
3. Where were you born? Cortland, New York
4. Where do you live now? Melbourne, Florida

5. What is your profession? Not working today; home healthcare

6. Did you read Donald Trump's 1987 book, *The Art of the Deal?* No

7. Did you hate Donald Trump before he was elected president—in other words, on day one of his presidency? No, not before he was president; I hate him now because I always thought he was fake and a phony, but he didn't have any impact on my life then as he does today.

8. Do you understand and support sanctuary cities? If yes, why? Yes, there needs to be a "safety net" under this new regime.

9. Do you believe the economy is better and stronger today than it was two years ago? No and we haven't felt the effects of the tariffs yet. I credit Obama for the economy.

10. What opinion do you have of loud, obnoxious New Yorkers? I don't feel they are loud and obnoxious as much as they don't accept any bulls**t.

11. Do you believe it was a mistake for Hillary Clinton to use a private email server for intra-government correspondence while she was secretary of state and that information could have ended up in the wrong hands? H***, no. This was a nothing burger, and her private email server was never hacked.

12. Do you believe Donald Trump is responsible for the current economy, GDP, and low unemployment rate? No. Executive orders only and no policy. Wall Street is loving the deregulations.

13. Do you credit Donald Trump and his administration for the decimation of ISIS and the reduction of terror threats in America today? No
14. Do you believe Donald Trump has created the "great divide" in Washington politics today, or was it like that many years prior? This started under Obama because he was a black president. Republicans have always driven this great divide.
15. Do you believe our country and culture are facing numerous issues today? Yes
16. Do you believe "incremental change" or "drastic measures" are required to get things back on track? Drastic measures
17. Do you dislike people who voted for or support Donald Trump? No, but if they are still strong supporters, yes.

Allowed rant: "I was a lazy, d*** American who never voted prior. I never feared a past presidential nominee, but Donald Trump being on the ballot scared me into voting. He's a commie bastard, and the Helsinki summit was an embarrassment. I feel that I don't have a representative in Washington DC today in the likes of Donald Trump."

Interview 6: Mike, the husband
1. Age? 64
2. Sex? Male
3. Where were you born? Elmira, New York
4. Where do you live now? Melbourne, Florida
5. What is your profession? Field service engineer, electronics automation equipment

6. Did you read Donald Trump's 1987 book, *The Art of the Deal*? No

7. Did you hate Donald Trump before he was elected president—in other words, on day one of his presidency? No, but I wanted anybody but Trump.

8. Do you understand and support sanctuary cities? If yes, why? Unsure on this one, but anything Trump, I am suspicious of the agenda.

9. Do you believe the economy is better and stronger today than it was two years ago? Yes

10. What opinion do you have of loud, obnoxious New Yorkers? A very negative opinion.

11. Do you believe it was a mistake for Hillary Clinton to use a private email server for intragovernment correspondence while she was secretary of state and that information could have ended up in the wrong hands? Yes, but they all do it ten times worse.

12. Do you believe Donald Trump is responsible for the current economy, GDP, and low unemployment rate? No, it was already on its way up prior to his presidency.

13. Do you credit Donald Trump and his administration for the decimation of ISIS and the reduction of terror threats in America today? No

14. Do you believe that Donald Trump has created the "great divide" in Washington politics today, or was it like that many years prior? No, but he widened it. I've never seen it like this in my lifetime.

15. Do you believe our country and culture are facing numerous issues today? Yes

16. Do you believe "incremental change" or "drastic measures" are required to get things back on track? Incremental change

17. Do you dislike people who voted for or support Donald Trump? No, the people that voted for him were ignorant. If the people that voted for him are still strong supporters, I really question why.

Allowed rant: "I was a registered Republican prior to and on this election. For me, it was anybody but Trump. I changed my party affiliation one week after the election."

Interview 7: Marlene, "Philly Girl"

1. Age? 59
2. Sex? Female
3. Where were you born? Philadelphia, Pennsylvania
4. Where do you live now? Philadelphia, Pennsylvania
5. What is your profession? Marketing director for an international commercial real estate brokerage firm
6. Did you read Donald Trump's 1987 book, *The Art of the Deal*? No, and have no intention of ever doing so!
7. Did you hate Donald Trump before he was elected president—in other words, on day one of his presidency? Yes. I have never liked Donald Trump, the man, the celebrity, and especially the politician. Also, working in the commercial real estate space, I've encountered and worked with quite a few high-profile developers (like Trump) and know "his kind" all too well. I've also done business with "respectable" real estate professionals that have done business with Trump, and no one has ever had a good experience

professionally with him. They all say they'd "never do business with him again, that he's a crook and a slimeball." Most are Republicans, and they didn't vote for him because of their past experience with him.

8. Do you understand and support sanctuary cities? If yes, why? Yes. I understand sanctuary cities and live in Philadelphia, which is a sanctuary city. I don't know if I would say I support sanctuary cities 100 percent; however, I believe our law enforcement has much larger fish to fry than some poor illegal immigrant that is a law-abiding (with the exception of being illegal), hardworking individual doing all of the labor-intensive jobs that most lazy/entitled Americans feel are beneath them and would never do. I would much rather see us focus on the serious criminals in our cities—rapists/thieves/drug dealers—rather than detaining immigrants for being undocumented, living in our city most of their lives, causing no real threats to our communities.

9. Do you believe the economy is better and stronger today than it was two years ago? It is strong today, but it was stronger four years ago, pre-Trump. I don't credit Trump with the economic growth that is going on today. Our economy has been gaining strength over the past several years. If you are amongst the wealthiest of Americans (like Trump himself), he is certainly generating more value; however he is not doing a d*** thing for the average workers who need more assistance than those making billions a year that could easily handle a tax increase.

10. What opinion do you have of loud, obnoxious New Yorkers? I'm not a fan.

11. Do you believe it was a mistake for Hillary Clinton to use a private email server for intragovernment correspondence while she was secretary of state and that information could have ended up in the wrong hands? Yes. I believe that was a huge mistake, and given her position as the secretary of state, she should have (and I'm sure she did) known better. It was a totally shady move. We all have professional protocol, which we are well aware of and must follow, and that one, in my opinion, was just plain stupidity on her part.

12. Do you believe Donald Trump is responsible for the current economy, GDP, and low unemployment rate? Kind of answered this question in number eight.

13. Do you credit Donald Trump and his administration for the decimation of ISIS and the reduction of terror threats in America today? Not really sure. It's possible. Trump's a loose cannon. I think everyone should be afraid of him because there is no telling what he would/could do at any given moment . . . but, then again, it may have absolutely nothing to do with him.

14. Do you believe Donald Trump has created the "great divide" in Washington politics today, or was it like that many years prior? I don't believe he is helping the great divide; as a matter of fact, I think he is making it much worse, but I do believe this has been happening for many years.

15. Do you believe our country and culture are facing numerous issues today? Yes

16. Do you believe "incremental change" or "drastic measures" are required to get things back on track? I think we need drastic measures, but I'm not sure how many drastic measures will actually be carried out by this administration or even the next. So, incremental change is better than nothing. We just need change—period.

17. Do you dislike people who voted for or support Donald Trump? No. Everyone is entitled to their own opinions. I may not agree with many of their opinions, but I tend to be open-minded and understand why those that support Trump support him, but most supporters don't recognize his *many* flaws, which is what upsets me most.

Allowed rant: "I think the problem with politics today is Democrats and Republicans are both in the wrong. Neither is willing to come together for the greater good of this country and its people. I think both parties need to learn to work together, understand the challenges, and try to figure out how to solve the major issues at hand—rather than continuously canceling one another out and resolving nothing."

Interview 8: LOOP
1. Age? 64
2. Sex? Male
3. Where were you born? Chicago, Illinois
4. Where do you live now? Deerfield Beach, Florida
5. What is your profession? Retail business owner
6. Did you read Donald Trump's 1987 book, *The Art of the Deal*? Not all of it, a few chapters

7. Did you hate Donald Trump before he was elected president—in other words, on day one of his presidency? I knew him from various fund-raisers prior, and he referred to me as "Mr. Steinway." But, during the election process, yes, I hated the guy.

8. Do you understand and support sanctuary cities? If yes, why? No

9. Do you believe the economy is better and stronger today than it was two years ago? No

10. What opinion do you have of loud, obnoxious New Yorkers? I'm okay there. After all, I married one!

11. Do you believe it was a mistake for Hillary Clinton to use a private email server for intragovernment correspondence while she was secretary of state and that information could have ended up in the wrong hands? Yes. In business, you are typically given a device for that job and should use it. She didn't, and that was a mistake.

12. Do you believe Donald Trump is responsible for the current economy, GDP, and low unemployment rate? No, the economy has been moving forward. I can't give Trump all the credit.

13. Do you credit Donald Trump and his administration for the decimation of ISIS and the reduction of terror threats in America today? (long pause) I don't know. Not really sure that much has changed here.

14. Do you believe Donald Trump has created the "great divide" in Washington politics today, or was it like that many years prior? Yes

15. Do you believe our country and culture are facing numerous issues today? Yes

16. Do you believe "incremental change" or "drastic measures" are required to get things back on track? I believe we have more issues today and things are worse since Donald Trump became president. I believe that his administration has created the great divide.
17. Do you dislike people who voted for or support Donald Trump? No, but it's frustrating in trying to have a conversation with a Trump supporter.

Allowed rant: "I think Donald Trump is an a****** and real SOB. Maybe in the construction and building business you have to be rougher in how you deal with people. I believe that he can handle things like a gentleman behind closed doors rather than the way he talks to and treats people."

Interview 9: Paul, the son
1. Age? 31
2. Sex? Male
3. Where were you born? Binghamton, New York
4. Where do you live now? Binghamton, New York
5. What is your profession? High school social studies teacher
6. Did you read Donald Trump's 1987 book, *The Art of the Deal*? No
7. Did you hate Donald Trump before he was elected president—in other words, on day one of his presidency? I never had much of an opinion on him before his political days. Just thought he was another reality-TV guy. I started to dislike him during the GOP primaries. He made a mockery of the whole process, and it blew my mind that throughout the entire

primary and presidential election season, the press continued to give him endless free coverage, no matter how ridiculous he sounded. They didn't care about substance or covering someone that would actually be good for the country, like John Kasich. They were more concerned with their ratings, so they just talked Trump nonstop. I also couldn't understand why, no matter how many mistakes he made that normally would end any other candidacy, people didn't seem to care, and he only got more and more popular. He also never said anything of substance, and people ate it up. It bothers me to this day that the media never really pushed him on any issues. Nobody pressed him for specifics; they just let him make ridiculous claims and promises without any detail or data to back him up. I really blame the media for making Donald Trump a "legitimate" candidate.

8. Do you understand and support sanctuary cities? If yes, why? I understand them and partially support them. I agree with the idea of wanting illegal immigrants to come forward to report crimes and take advantage of public services (especially those with young family members) without fear of getting in trouble with immigration when they have done nothing wrong other than being here illegally. I do think that if any crime is committed, they need to be reported.

9. Do you believe the economy is better and stronger today than it was two years ago? First of all, to give a president *sole* credit for a struggling or booming economy is ridiculous. There are so many factors that go into economic growth beyond what one president

can do. I get annoyed when Trump makes claims that the economy is growing because of him. It isn't. To answer the question, yes, the economy is stronger today. But, the economy was trending that way under President Obama's administration. I believe most of what Trump has offered the economy is the "illusion" of being pro-jobs and pro-growth. I don't think being two years into his term is enough time for his policies to really have set in to have a major impact on the economy.

10. What opinion do you have of loud, obnoxious New Yorkers? I don't care. I lived in New York City for a few years, and my wife is from Long Island, so I have spent a lot of time down that way, and it is what it is. You get those type of people anywhere. Not all New Yorkers fit that stereotype, and Donald Trump being a New Yorker has nothing to do with me disliking him.

11. Do you believe it was a mistake for Hillary Clinton to use a private email server for intragovernment correspondence while she was secretary of state and that information could have ended up in the wrong hands? I do, but she is not the only one who does it. I think the GOP and media made much more of it than they should have. The fact that people were more upset about the private server than anything Trump did (sexual assault allegations, *Access Hollywood* tape, "Mexican rapists," making fun of the handicapped, bullying, etc.) is very troubling and doesn't reflect well on our country.

12. Do you believe Donald Trump is responsible for the current economy, GDP, and low unemployment rate?

No. As I said in a previous answer, there is a lot more that goes into the economy/GDP/UR than what a single president does. I do think the idea of him being good for the economy has helped, but he inherited a growing economy from Obama's years. (Again, not totally Obama's doing, but his administration at least had eight years to implement government policy that did have an impact on the economy.) I can't name any specific policies that Trump's administration has put into place that would have helped the economy this soon. The tax cut, for example, is still too young to really have had any major impact on economic data, in my opinion—potentially in another year or two, though. I do think that there are a lot of things he is doing that he thinks will be good for the economy that is not. Mainly his rolling back of environmental protections. I strongly disagree with the impact that will have on the economy and am very worried about the negative impacts it will have on our planet and health. Sacrificing the environment in the name of economic growth is not good policy. I strongly disagree with the prevailing GOP idea that it's one or the other when, in fact, sustainability/environmental protection and economic growth can and should go hand in hand.

13. Do you credit Donald Trump and his administration for the decimation of ISIS and the reduction of terror threats in America today? No. Like the economy, Trump is benefiting from policies put into place by Obama. I credit Trump with continuing to put pressure on ISIS, but Obama did a lot, too.

14. Do you believe Donald Trump has created the "great divide" in Washington politics today, or was it like that many years prior? I don't think he created it. I think there already was a strong political divide in our country. I do think he used it to his advantage and rose to power through that strong divide. I definitely think he has made it worse and has continued to divide rather than bring us together.

15. Do you believe our country and culture are facing numerous issues today? Yes

16. Do you believe "incremental change" or "drastic measures" are required to get things back on track? I am very concerned for our country. It really concerns me that someone like Donald Trump with all that he has done and all that he has said can get elected POTUS. He has totally destroyed the image of the POTUS and is as far from being "presidential" as I have ever seen. As a teacher and father who is trying to instill good values and morals in my students and daughter, it makes me sick to see and hear the things he does. He is such a horrible example for our future generations. He is everything we tell our kids not to be. Yet, there he is—elevated to the highest office in the country and millions of people loving everything he says and does. I am also very concerned with where our culture is going—and that is what has allowed Trump to thrive. The culture of not caring about sexual assault allegations, demeaning women, discriminating against certain Americans, violating human rights, destroying the environment, etc., is rampant in our country right now and has me very concerned and

scared for our future. I recently became a father (my daughter is four months old currently), and I am so worried about the world she will be growing up in and the state of the country and planet that we will be leaving behind for her and others. While I am not a huge fan of the Democratic Party all of the time, I think they need a big win in the midterms to restore some balance to the country. I don't think it is ever good to have one party controlling all three branches of government which Republicans/conservatives now do.

17. Do you dislike people who voted for or support Donald Trump? I don't dislike them; I just don't understand them. I don't understand how you could ever vote for or continue to support someone who has said and done the things he has. There were some strong GOP candidates that got passed over by Trump's sideshow, and I don't get it. I have my theories as to why people support him, and that makes me worried for our country. I also think these people are not getting the proper information on Trump and his policies. They rely on fake news, Trump's outright lies, and Fox News for their information and refuse to investigate the other side. This is true of liberals as well. I think it is a real problem in the world right now that we need to address. We have too many uninformed citizens and people who vote blindly by party rather than investigating the truth and choosing the best candidate. And there is too much misinformation and lies out there for people to get a good handle on the truth. It is something that my fellow teachers and I

struggle with every day—teaching kids to find and analyze multiple sources in pursuit of the truth. It is not easy for me to do it all of the time. Turn on Fox News and you hear one thing; then change to MSNBC and you hear something completely different. You have to really work to find the truth, and not everyone is able or willing to do that. And it doesn't help when nobody holds people in power accountable for what they say.

Allowed rant: "Donald Trump can say anything he wants (and he does), regardless of how true or false it is, and people will just believe it. All I can do is laugh when he says things like, 'I never said that,' and there are videos of him saying that exact thing. But the scary thing is that people will just believe that he never said it. It's a troubling time in our country right now, and I am very worried."

Summary

I compiled the interviews but at no time did I add any information or distort the answers. I believe the interviewees enjoyed the process as it allowed them some much-needed venting. I interviewed nine people, of whom five were women and four were men, aged from thirty-one to seventy-one. This was a fairly balanced group of individuals, half I had never met before. Their professions varied from a retail business owner, teacher, hostess, and even ex-military. None of them had read Donald Trump's book *The Art of the Deal*. An interesting point is that one of the interviewees thought this question was to confirm the credibility of Donald Trump when that is not why I asked the question at all. I asked this question because I reasoned that if they had read the book, they would have better identified with his demeanor.

The opinions were well balanced so far as hating Donald Trump prior to taking office. Regarding the question of the economy, most interviewees did not attribute this to President Trump. Most felt the economy was on its way up prior to his presidency. In one instance, an interviewee answered yes, it was better; however, he predicted a great crash is lurking under President Trump. For the question regarding Hillary Clinton's email server and whether or not she handled this properly or not, everyone but one person agreed that this was a mistake. Most of the interviewees elaborated, however, after acknowledging this as a mistake.

The question of military and terrorist activity today was an interesting one for me. By a very large margin, people did not think we were any safer today than under President Obama. The surprise to me, personally, was that I know of a lot of people who are traveling to Europe again or for the very first time in their lives and feeling safer under the current administration and its policies. Regarding Donald Trump being responsible for the great divide in our country today, it seems everyone agreed that we were divided prior; however, they feel it has become worse and more permanent under the current president.

The last question of my interview was rather entertaining for me personally: "Do you dislike people who voted for or support Donald Trump?" In every instance, there was a very long pause before their answer. Across the board, the answer was predominantly no but, again, with exception. In one instance, Steth said, "As a group, yes; individually, no." Those interviewed have problems today with family members and friends who are Trump supporters, and this question really seemed to hone in on the great divide.

The rants were to allow interviewees to add any other comments, and this was also quite entertaining as these seemed to reveal the real hatred toward Donald J. Trump. Here's a sample of those comments: arrogant, a cheater, offends minorities, flaming a******, selfish man, doesn't show a human side, has destroyed people's lives, narcissist, liar, sociopath, wants to be a dictator, money launderer, brought about racism, real SOB. Notable quotes include, he "will never be my president," and "Donald Trump being on the ballot scared me into voting for the very first time," and "I changed my party affiliation one week after this past election."

It seems those who hate Donald J. Trump will find any excuse to rationalize their hatred toward this guy. It's no different than how those who support Donald J. Trump and his policies rationalize their reasons to support him. The next chapter delves into this perspective a bit further. Read on.

CHAPTER 18

Inside the Mind of the Author

Now you have the opportunity to judge me. Although I'm certain that my opinions were apparent from other chapters, I actually decided to add this chapter in after completing all of my interviews in the prior chapter. I better understand the feelings of the haters and it allowed me to better reflect on my own opinions from a better perspective. It's true that I cringe when certain politicians speak a single word, so I understand how the other side must feel. Nancy Pelosi, Hillary Clinton, Chuck Schumer, Maxine Waters, and certain other politicians make my skin crawl when they say *anything*. Admittedly, I am "profiling" these particular politicians in a very negative way. Even if they have a novel concept or idea to bring to Washington, I admit I am already in shutdown mode. It must be the same for the Trump haters regarding all of his accomplishments to date. However, that list is very long, so I'm not sure how spin could be put on every single accomplishment to put him in such a negative light.

It's almost unfathomable to ponder what things would be like without obstruction. How much stronger would our country and its great citizens be without discord? Would the long list of accomplishments be even that much longer? Consider the drama surrounding our president's Supreme Court nominee, Brett Kavanaugh. Chuck Schumer and others were obstructing his pick before Kavanaugh was even nominated for the post. What were they thinking, other than simply not wanting to support a single decision this president makes?

Think about that opposition for a minute. This would imply that the Democratic Congress and Senate, as well as the liberal media, are immediately against half of our country. After all, half the country voted for and support this president. Does the opposition not support a single thing the current president wants to accomplish, even if it means securing borders, enforcing laws that have been on the books for many years, and keeping Americans safe? Rather than support this president's safety measures, the Democrats and liberal media will claim this president is racist and stir such distractions rather than doing their jobs.

As I write on October 22, 2018, a huge caravan is headed to our southern border from Central America. Isn't this the perfect opportunity for an ISIS terrorist, MS-13 gang member, or other "bad guy" to enter our country? Simply put, the "right way" and "wrong way" to enter the United States of America has been defined. Why would the Democrats support the wrong way?

The Democratic Party and many of their leaders were playing dirty politics well before we got to where we're at today. Debra Wasserman Schultz was head of the DNC when emails were leaked in July, 2016, that showed the committee was actively trying to undermine Bernie Sanders's presidential campaign. They targeted his religion, claiming he was an atheist and said he had "no understanding" of their party. A special fund was created for Hillary Clinton and the more than twenty thousand leaked emails showed this bias. Shultz later resigned, and Donna Brazile took over as interim chairperson.

So, to keep this momentum and bias toward Hillary Clinton going strong, Donna Brazile actually tipped off Clinton's campaign about the Flint water crisis and other questions the day before her primary debate with Bernie Sanders on April 14, 2016. On October 11, 2016, she lied about it, claiming she never had access to the debate questions beforehand. On October 14 of that year, Brazile was fired from CNN. Brazile later admitted to sharing the questions, and on November 7, 2016, she claimed she had no regrets over this.

She went on to say that if she were to do it all over again, she would make sure she knew a lot more about cybersecurity ahead of time. She later admitted that the Democratic primary was rigged against Bernie Sanders, and I suppose that makes for good reading in a new book she has released.

I'm not making this stuff up here. A lawsuit was ultimately filed against the DNC by donors, on allegations of rigging the primary against Sanders. On August 25, 2017, Federal Judge William Zloch dismissed the lawsuit. The court actually conceded that the DNC had the right to rig the primaries against Sanders.

So, even within their own party, the attacks were desperate and ugly, doing whatever it might take to win. Now that these primaries and the general election are long behind them, the Democratic Party's ugly attention and corruption turn to our now president as they do whatever it takes to foil his success. Ugly politics and people at their very worst.

It was my hope that a one-party majority, meaning a Republican president, Congress, and Senate, would be able to accomplish things for America today as both parties seem to vote straight down the line. The days of going across the street to the local pub and working out differences seem to be long gone. Who knows, maybe if they had their own version of "The Duck Tavern" across the street from the Capitol building, with happy hour each day from three to seven, things would be different. (Local pub owners in the DC area, please take note of this little gem in East Boca Raton, serving over one hundred beers from around the world and live music on weekends.) The Democratic Party even seems to want to incite violence or aggressive tactics regarding their mission, which could encourage another civil war. I'm a simple facts kind of guy, so let's take a peek at some comments leading into the 2018 midterm elections:

- Former Attorney General Eric Holder (D): Urging Democrats to shed the sentiment of Michelle Obama's,

"When they go low, we go high," Holder said. "When they go low, we kick them."

- Former Secretary of State Hillary Clinton (D): "Democrats cannot be civil toward Republicans." She also said, "How can we be civil when our opponents are trying to take away everything we stand for?"
- Representative Maxine Waters (D): In June of 2018, she called on her supporters to publicly confront and harass members of the Trump administration in response to the zero tolerance policy that led to the separation of families at the border, saying, "Let's make sure we show up wherever we have to show up. And if you see anybody from that cabinet in a restaurant, in a department store, at a gasoline station, you get out and you create a crowd. And you push back on them. And you tell them they're not welcome anymore, anywhere."
- Former speaker of the House, Nancy Pelosi (D): "Trump's daily lack of civility has provoked responses predictable but unacceptable."

Such incivility had Representative Steve Scalise (R) nearly shot to death in June of 2017; Senator Rand Paul (R) attacked by a neighbor in June, 2018; Sarah Huckabee Sanders (press secretary) banned from a restaurant in June of 2018; Florida AG Pam Bondi confronted by protesters at a movie theater in June, 2018; and more. Michelle Obama actually rebuked the Holder and Clinton comments, seeming to be the only adult in the room. She's always had class and is obviously in disagreement with incivility.

Even when such a historic trade deal is accomplished between the three North American countries after twenty-five years, all that the Democrats and press wanted to cover was the Brett Kavanaugh Supreme Court hearing. His drinking at college parties over thirty years ago was highlighted and allegations of sexual misconduct were raised, though not corroborated. So, I ponder that situation as well. The Democrats and liberal news outlets today *are* obstructing. Unsubstantiated information had the people who hated Trump's pick rip-roaring mad. The plan was to try and get this justice pick delayed until after the midterms, hoping that the Democrats might have taken over the House by then. Doctor Ford's testimony and the seventh FBI check into allegations and witness interviews added additional delays but didn't derail the pick as Democrats had planned. Those who hope to obstruct Trump's plans and policies will have to regroup and figure out their next plan of attack.

For me, this is vile. I've voted in every presidential election and primary for at least the last forty years, and my picks have won less than 50 percent of the time. It doesn't mean I have taken to the streets to attack the opposition party's members. This behavior is completely unacceptable; I don't understand it. I can only surmise that our interpersonal skills have gone to s**t with texting, social media, and other communication technology changes.

I will make no excuses for myself; I have always told it like it is and am a very open and transparent person. And, because of this trait, which I date back to my preteen years, I know how to communicate with others. Many today, however, do not. I have to believe that the people causing such a raucous today don't know any better. That's the only explanation I can surmise. If one wasn't happy with the pricing of a particular product in a grocery store, I can't imagine he would pick up that product and sling it at the store manager. Such behavior would be ridiculous.

And, regarding the Brett Kavanaugh nomination, I suppose I have a comment or two on that. Who remembers their college parties? Really? Witnesses were asked about what they remember from a specific party or parties from over thirty years ago. Dr. Ford wasn't credible to me and really seemed to be a woman with issues. She admittedly had anxiety and other disorders that were diagnosed and discussed at the hearing. And regarding these college parties, I'm certain grain alcohol punch was there, just as when I went to college. Large amounts of alcohol were consumed at some of these events, for sure. And, except for Bill Clinton, I'm sure people were inhaling as well.

And, regarding the Supreme Court nominee not having any political bias. Really? You're d*** right there is bias. Isn't that why the Democrats were so pissed off in the first place? Only two types of justices can be elected: one, a fundamentalist following the laws of the Constitution, typically conservative; or two, a justice who rules from the bench, interpreting the Constitution as to what it might mean today, typically liberal. I'm sure we can all agree to disagree here, but isn't that why most of the rulings in the Supreme Court pass by a very narrow vote since they have been so split between liberal- and conservative-minded judges?

And what of the Democrats playing the Dr. Ford card the day before the vote on Kavanaugh? Coincidence? I don't think so. What I do think, however, is that the Me Too movement has had a bit of a setback as this witness had prior issues with anxiety disorders and recollection of events. Her testimony could possibly influence the outcome for those who come forward in the future. Pure political gaming. Very sad.

When I see that at least six large American companies (Ford, Dow, Sprint, Chevrolet, Carrier, and IBM) reinvested in America following President Trump's election, this makes me proud. As well, a Pentagon report issued on October 5, 2018, said they would be expanding direct investment in US industries vital to national security. These sectors include scarce materials, Alane fuel cells, lithium sea water batteries, propellers, and other products.

As a kid growing up in the 60s, I knew "Made in the USA" was a very proud slogan and symbol, and it represented 92 percent of goods sold in this country then. The president-elect wasn't my first choice; however, I was extremely interested in and supportive of many of his promises, including bringing jobs and manufacturing back to the United States. I've been in the electronics manufacturing sector since 1982, so this issue really strikes a chord for me personally. Is it because we have outsourced so much for so long that kids today cannot identify with *that* America, which seems so long ago? Just as I cannot blame the family who has been on an entitlement program like welfare for decades, I find it difficult to blame those who might not know that we truly were a better country in the 60s and 70s.

CHAPTER 19

Only History Will Tell

In my late twenties in the early 80s, I was traveling to the United Kingdom quite frequently for business. I would take side trips to Paris, the French Riviera, and Munich and was traveling across the United States at that time as well. Ronald Reagan was our fortieth president and in office during this time, from 1981 to 1989, but not well liked globally. Back in those days, you had very few TV stations to choose from, especially in the United Kingdom. Actually, there were only three to choose from, and I typically watched CNN International for the news. I also watched a local British station and *Spitting Image*, a satirical puppet show. The show actually won two Emmy awards back in 1985 and 1986 in the popular arts category. The episodes were very funny, and I would encourage you to google "*Spitting Image* and President Reagan brains."

The world was weary of President Reagan because they feared he had one hand on the nuke button and didn't have any brains. For my international travel and dealing with so many managers in foreign offices, our conversations often turned to American politics as they couldn't quite figure Reagan out. They made fun of Reagan constantly, and it's truly interesting to me that Ronald Reagan is now revered as one of the best American presidents of all time, with memorable contributions such as "Reaganomics." Let's take a quick peek at some of President Reagan's most famous quotes:

- "Government's first duty is to protect the people, not run their lives."
- "There are no great limits to growth because there are no limits of human intelligence, imagination, and wonder."
- "There are no constraints on the human mind, no walls around the human spirit, no barriers to our progress except those we ourselves erect."
- "The objective I propose is quite simple to state: to foster the infrastructure of democracy—the system of a free press, unions, political parties, universities—which allows a people to choose their own way to develop their own culture, to reconcile their own differences through peaceful means."
- "If we love our country, we should also love our countrymen."

- "When you can't make them see the light, make them feel the heat."
- "If we ever forget that we are One Nation Under God, then we will be a nation gone under."

Ronald Reagan was a Hollywood actor and trade union leader until becoming governor of California in 1977. He was raised in a poor family in Illinois and graduated from Eureka College in 1932. He moved to Hollywood in 1937, and after acting in a few major productions, he became the president of the Screen Actors Guild, the labor union for actors. He was a Democrat until 1962. Five years later, his political career began as governor of California, and by then, he was a conservative and Republican. At the time of his presidency, Reagan implemented sweeping new political and economic initiatives. He reduced taxes, spawned economic growth, favored economic deregulation, increased military spending, and spurred the war on drugs.

Comparing President Trump to President Reagan uncovers uncanny similarities, with two major differences. President Reagan had a softer demeanor and was gentlemanlike, no matter the circumstances. President Trump is more abrasive on the surface, but he's trying to accomplish the same things.

The second difference has more to do with a difference in culture between the 80s and today. Hate-fueled stories now fill our TVs and social media outlets. Facebook brings people together to share their opinions around the clock. So, if we examine the days that Reagan was president, with limited cable stations, no internet, no social media, and no smartphone, and then compare it to our information resources now, the difference is clear. What if all of these tools were available to us then? How much more might we have known about the inner workings of Reagan's White House and his personal life?

So, how will President Trump and his economic policies look in the history books twenty years from now? Will his legacy be about porn stars, Russian collusion, rigged elections, and tweets? Or, will his military, economic, and social policies be examined for the broader impact they had on all Americans? Will the historians note that this president left the world a better place—or worse—than when he entered office? When all the hate dust settles, I believe we will be left with only the facts of his one- or two-term legacy.

Only time will tell if he had a drastic impact on the divisiveness in our country. I don't know Donald Trump, but by living in Boca Raton, Florida, for thirty-four years, I know a heck of a lot of New Yorkers. As a whole, this group of people is not shy. They are rather transparent and tell it like it is, whether you want to hear it or not. They are loud and enjoy being amongst friends who are louder than they are. They are also a strong-willed people, very intelligent, and generally successful.

So, while the president is currently judged more on his personality than his accomplishments, I will be interested to see what history will say. With any change, there is resistance. As he is changing a lot of things, resistance is high.

Will historians look back and write books on the division—the extreme optimism and pessimism—of 2018? It seems the optimists are those who support Trump's ideas, trusting even better things will happen tomorrow. In contrast, the pessimists are those who seek to undermine the sitting president, no matter what; they are expecting worse things to happen tomorrow because they do not believe in the man or his ideas for a better America. While the president's slogan was "Make America Great Again," Governor Andrew Cuomo (D) of New York stated on August 16, 2018, that "America was never that great."

I believe history will prove that young people, millennials, and others who did not support Trump got more involved in politics than ever before. It will also show that he brought more attention to policy issues and sanctuary cities and actually forced Americans to become educated on such topics. And, history will tell of people paying more attention to the news than before, which compelled them to vote and participate in various election cycles.

CHAPTER 20

"Make America Great Again"

Times have truly changed in our country, even since I was a kid. Back in the 60s and 70s, we played outside for hours, went to the creek to go fishing or crabbing with buddies, camped out in the backyard, drank water right from the garden hose, and got a good whipping when we deserved it. We respected our elders and teachers, called everyone Mr. or Mrs., and didn't sue our parents for nonsense. All those who are fifty years old or older grew up in these simpler times. And I have no regrets for that nun whipping my butt with a paddle in front of the entire class in fourth grade. I deserved it and learned my lesson. My parents are now deceased, but I don't begrudge them a single punishment or whipping they gave me. I earned them, for sure.

I often wonder if future generations will have the same childhood and opportunities I had back then. Lyndon B. Johnson was president when I was seven. He was an independent and ran for the Democratic Party against Barry Goldwater. Other US presidents during my childhood years included Dwight Eisenhower (R), John F. Kennedy (D), and Richard Nixon (R). These men were in office until I was sixteen years old or so. My childhood memories were fun-filled as we camped out in each other's backyards, went fishing or crabbing before the crack of dawn, had backyard barbecues, went down to the local fields to play baseball or football, played kickball, went bike riding, went exploring in the woods, drove mini bikes in the woods, and enjoyed dozens of outdoor activities with friends.

When it came time for certain holidays, like the Fourth of July, Memorial Day, Columbus Day, Veterans Days, or Flag Day, we couldn't wait to help our dads hang the American flag in our yards or on the porch. My dad had a very large flagpole that he would attach to the fence in our yard to hoist the flag. We lived in a corner row house, so the flag could be seen from all vantage points; Dad really enjoyed that. We'd hoist the flag and then just stare at it for a while. Our parents were so very proud of America; thus, their children shared these same feelings. We cherished going to parades or singing the national anthem at football and baseball games, and we were truly proud to be Americans.

I wasn't born into a wealthy family; we weren't able to buy new bikes every year or a brand-new car every couple of years. Therefore, I truly appreciate what I have now, knowing I earned it. I will be forever grateful for living in a country that has provided me incredible opportunity for success and the chance to meet so many wonderful people along the way. When you have to earn what you have, you appreciate things that much more. I speak from a position of experience, having two children who have grown up with a very different lifestyle than I did.

Things have come so much easier for them, and it makes it a little harder for them to truly appreciate what they've been given. They've also grown up with a different national culture. Take, for example, cursing. I have two absolutely wonderful children, don't get me wrong here. I just can't imagine saying things to or around my parents that kids do and say today. The concept of respect is very different, and the same goes for respect toward teachers, coaches, or any other adult. I see many kids today simply calling adults by their first name. Might seem a bit trite, but I see these cultural changes around us every day of our lives.

Why do people attack the slogan "Make America Great Again"? Meghan McCain, speaking at her dad's funeral on September 1, 2018, said, "The America of John McCain has no need to be made great again because America was always great." It seems, at every turn, our president, who recognizes the same challenges I see, will meet resistance to what he is attempting to accomplish. Why? During his inaugural address on January 20, 1961, John F. Kennedy delivered an inspirational speech that addressed what it is to be an American, including main themes of freedom, peace, God's role in our lives, service to others, and personal accountability. He said, "Ask not what your country can do for you but what you can do for your country." I ask, where are these same values at today? What have we become? Why are things so different culturally?

I believe that the president's rallying cry to "Make America Great Again" is not something he intended for just one person but for all to adhere to. This charter, this mission, requires change throughout the culture as we remember where we have come from, understand what we have endured to get where we are, and reclaim the values we once had. We can all nitpick his motto to death: "Make America Better," "Make America Great," "Make Our America Great Again," and so forth. However, for those Americans who truly believe we were once better than we are today, it's up to each of us to contribute to making America a country we can all be proud of and to show the world we are still a beacon of hope and leadership. We are a vast melting pot of people of different national origins who settled all across our great land. We should not be ashamed if we are rich or poor, black or white, if we drive a Maserati or don't drive at all. We should be very proud of who we are and where we are from.

Earlier in my career, I had the fortune of working for a very large British company with factories in England and Scotland. I was a senior manager for operations in the United States and would travel to the United Kingdom quite often for business. On one such trip, management told me a senior executive for this $7 billion company wanted to meet with me. Specifically, he wanted to meet on Friday afternoon. He knew I was frustrated and had ideas for strategies we should implement in the United States market.

As I sat in his modest office with furniture that seemed to be three hundred years old, he looked at me and said, "You Americans just don't get it. You're always striving to be number one, in first place." I replied, "But, yes, of course we do." He looked me straight in the eye and said, "It's a lot safer to be second than it is to be in first place." That's a very profound statement that has stuck with me to this day. It's absolutely true.

In the early 80s, during the personal computer boom, all the companies were focused on IBM as they were number one. It's extremely hard to be in first place at anything, let alone to maintain that position for so many years. Whether we look at the automobile industry, sports teams, or technology companies, the baton has been passed along the way. As a country, we have truly been in first place for so long that it seems we've become complacent with that position. We shouldn't have to apologize for our stature on the world stage. We should be proud of who and what we are.

So, let's acknowledge some of the great inventions our young country of just 242 years has brought to this world:

- The Ferris wheel debuted at the Chicago World Fair on June 21, 1931. It was invented by George Washington Gale Ferris.
- The chocolate chip cookie was actually invented by accident in 1930 by Ruth Graves Wakefield, owner of the Toll House Inn in Whitman, Massachusetts.
- The zipper was invented in 1913 by Gideon Sundback and was actually a byproduct of the earlier clasp locker that was invented by Whitcomb L. Judson in 1893.

- The hearing aid was invented in 1902 by Miller Reese Hutchinson, an inventor from Alabama.
- The traffic light was invented in 1912 by Lester Wire, a policeman in Salt Lake City. (It originally had only red and green lights.)
- The microwave oven is now commonplace in most kitchens and was invented in 1945 by Percy Spencer, an engineer from Maine. This appliance was invented by accident. Percy was working on the magnetron for radar sets at Raytheon when he realized microwaves melted the chocolate in his pocket.
- The assembly line is a systematic, sequential method of producing goods; it's cost-effective since it lessens mistakes and hastens production time. The original concept was developed in 1901 by Ransom Olds at his motor vehicle company in Michigan. But the assembly line that left the most lasting influence on the manufacturing world was that of the Model T Ford by Henry Ford in 1908.
- Light emitting diodes (LEDs) were invented in 1962 by Nick Holonyak Jr., a consulting scientist at General Electric Company in Syracuse, New York.
- The global positioning system (GPS) was developed in 1973 by the US Department of Defense; however, it became fully operational in 1994. The global navigation satellite system is actually managed by the government of the United States. Though it was intended primarily for military use, we take advantage of the system through our mobile devices and navigational systems in vehicles today.

- The video game was invented in 1948 by Thomas T. Goldsmith Jr. and Estle Ray Mann. This first game was a cathode-ray-tube amusement device that allowed interaction between user and device with video feedback.
- Email was invented in 1971 by Ray Tomlinson, using ARPANET. The first email was sent using two computers side by side. Ray is also credited with using the ampersand (@) sign to separate the user's name and the user's machine (which later became the domain name). Where would we be without this? Sorry, sis. (My sister has worked for the US Postal Service for thirty-four years now, and I'm certain that if it weren't for that junk mail that fills our boxes daily, she would have had a different career.)
- The mobile phone was invented in 1973 by Dr. Martin Cooper, a vice president at Motorola Corporation. He actually led the development team that showcased the first one-kilogram mobile phone that year.
- The invention of the personal computer has a very long development history, although the first real PC was launched in the early 80s. While certain innovations are credited to the genius of Steve Jobs and Steve Wozniak of Apple, the development of the computer spans centuries. The modern digital computer's roots actually date back to 1937 to George Stibitz, who worked at the famous Bell Labs. But its widespread use occurred in the early 80s, and IBM, based right here in Boca Raton, Florida, contributed to this part of history. While the Apple boys certainly contributed to the early history of PC invention, it was actually a

man by the name of Dr. Philip Don Estridge who led the development team of the original IBM personal computer, which changed the computer industry and vastly increased PC sales. Sadly, Dr. Estridge and his wife Mary Ann were killed in a plane crash, Delta Air Lines Flight 191, that flew from Ft. Lauderdale to Dallas/Fort Worth on August 2, 1985. He was just forty-eight years old. At the time of his death, the IBM ESD Division in Boca Raton had ten thousand employees and had sold over one million PCs.

- The internet is a network of networks that was formally introduced with the Internet Protocol Suite of the National Science Foundation in 1982, funded by the US Government.

Other great American inventions include dental floss (1815), defibrillator paddles (1947), the crash test dummy (1949), the laser (1960), and chemotherapy (1940). And many other inventions could be listed, for sure, but you can see the impact American inventions and ingenuity have had on the world. So, each in his own way, let's do our part to make this country great again and continue to bring inventions and ideas for the betterment of people around the planet. It starts at home, and it starts with you and me.

I suppose what surprises me most is that many Trump naysayers either believe America was always great or that it never was great to begin with. At its core, either train of thought seems not to want to give this particular president any credit for progress that "Make(s) America Great Again."

CHAPTER 21

~~My~~ (Our) President Has Balls!™

At the beginning of this book, I claimed to write about two things: changes in our American culture over the last four to five decades and the division in our country. Clearly, our democracy is in crisis mode. After conducting the interviews featured in chapter 17, I doubt that many, if any, Trump haters accept President Donald Trump as leader of our great country, able to take on the challenges facing our democracy. Just as those who support Donald Trump might justify in their own way what really went down with Vladimir

Putin at their meeting in Helsinki on July 16, 2018, I suppose those who oppose Trump added yet one more reason to get rid of this guy.

In his first five hundred days in office, President Donald J. Trump has achieved numerous results, both domestically and internationally. He has strengthened American leadership, security, and prosperity. The American economy is stronger; the American worker is experiencing more opportunities; confidence is soaring; and business is booming. President Trump has reasserted America's leadership on the world stage, approved the largest military/defense spending bill in history, and stood up against threats to national security. This president has certainly put the American people first and made our government more accountable.

As I write, over five hundred sanctuary jurisdictions are in the United States, and sixty-seven million people do not speak English. That represents one in every five people or *21 percent of our population.* My grandparents came to this country from Italy and did not speak English at the time, but they learned the language of the country they ultimately called home. Thus, protecting illegals in this country, allowing safe harbors, and letting them live here without the need to learn our language is very puzzling to me. If communication is the single-most-important asset a person has, why wouldn't this portion of the population even want to learn the language? Wouldn't both Democrats and Republicans support policies to help this population learn the English language and get ahead in our country?

While we recognize the United States is a great melting pot for different cultures, I'm concerned for our democracy, our values, our religious beliefs, and even our language as all are coming under fire. If one in every five people in this country doesn't speak English, how then can they understand or even relate to our culture and beliefs? I have traveled to many different countries and always bring two important things with me on every trip:

1. The understanding that I am an ambassador of my country, representing the United States of America. The people I meet will form an opinion of me, and I want this to be positive on behalf of all Americans.
2. Foreign language dictionaries and travel books (Rick Steve's are my absolute favorites) to learn about the food, culture, and language so I can respect that country, culture, and people.

I certainly can't imagine moving to France and not learning the language, the culture, what is accepted, and what is taboo.

If we can agree on one thing today, perhaps it would be that we have never witnessed such an election or such division in this country. While I respect the opinions and comments of every person I interviewed, I feel their comments represent a good sample of how Trump haters feel in this country. I simply do not respect how past politicians are getting in the way of our current president's negotiations with foreign countries, including adversaries. I don't support how the highest level of personnel within our FBI, CIA, and even the White House might be trying to undermine a sitting president.

We are all certainly entitled to our opinions; however, in close elections in the recent past, I never recall such outrage and daily attacks or insiders trying to undermine the president. Such rancor is absolutely undermining democracy and putting our very lives in danger. Since I believe the Trump haters outweigh by a large margin the Trump nonsupporters, I truly don't believe that this is their perspective. I believe that they see every action he takes as an absolute threat to our democracy and a hidden agenda for the wealthiest of Americans, and therefore reason it's okay if these insiders are trying to take him down.

On September 7, 2018, former President Barack Obama spoke at the University of Illinois, Urbana-Champaign, Illinois. Those with differing points of view may have different takeaways, but mine was the statement that Trump couldn't fix forty years of problems in his eight years of office. Incredible. Who else heard that? That's been the point of my book entirely. Democrats discuss seismic shifts in our government and democracy today, referring to Trump. Really? Is the real reason because we've been going off the rails for so many years now?

We have a president trying to fix many broken things quickly; thus, he encounters major pushback. He has the @%&! to do so, unlike his predecessors. After the eight years of the Obama presidency and what has been happening with respect to American culture, Americans were looking for a tough candidate to make some very tough decisions with respect to our economy, US jobs, immigration laws, potential terror and nuclear threats, and our culture. Many Americans were feeling abandoned as President Obama had spent eight years telling Americans that we are imperialists and going on apology tours country after country. We were afraid for what we had become and didn't want to continue on this negative spiral.

I apologize for this statement ahead of time, but, in short, we didn't want a wussy leading our country anymore. So, what, then, of Donald J. Trump? He's never seen a deal he couldn't make or a project he couldn't build. Everything done to date has been done big. Everything Trump does is bold.

Take, for example, his former airline, Trump Shuttle. I had the privilege of flying the Trump Shuttle on numerous business trips from LaGuardia Airport in New York City to Logan Airport in Boston. Donald Trump and Frank Lorenzo, the president of Eastern Airlines, met at a party in 1988, and Trump subsequently bought the shuttle from Eastern for $365 million. His investment was about providing luxury service while also marketing the Trump name. The shuttle had previously offered no-frills service from Eastern, but Trump promised to build a luxury airline. I can attest that he did just that. It was incredible.

The aircraft were painted in white livery, and the interiors were decorated with maple wood veneer, chrome seat belt latches, and gold-colored lavatory fixtures. The entire shuttle was like being in a first-class cabin. When you approached the gate at the airport, an attractive secretary was available to type a letter or offer any assistance you might need for your trip. Laptop computers were available to rent, and the shuttle was an early adopter of the GTE Airfone in-flight telephone system. Once onboard, complementary meals and champagne, beer, and wine were served. It was the Trump way, and it was done big. The airline venture was short-lived, lasting about four years. Jet fuel prices nearly doubled in 1990, due to our invasion of Kuwait. Costs of running the airline kept rising, and it was ultimately shut down in 1992.

Although the airline project ultimately failed, it demonstrated how Trump behaves. He doesn't do things half-a****.

So, when we elected this guy president, I assume many reasoned his approach to the critical issues facing our country would not be half-a**** either. However, challenges also come with this type of persona; expectations are high for all of those who surround him. After all, Donald Trump is one person, and the American people number 326 million. Most of us wanted an unapologetic president more than we wanted a constitutional conservative. We wanted a leader who wouldn't back down in a fight or draw new red lines.

If we examine what this president has done for the American economy alone, we cannot deny these facts:

- Nearly four million jobs have been created under President Trump's pro-growth agenda.
- Over 400,000 manufacturing jobs have been created, and manufacturing employment is at its highest level since December 2008; over 327,000 jobs were added in the twelve-month period between August, 2017 and August, 2018, the largest gain since 1995 (re: 345,000 manufacturing jobs were added).
- 367,000 construction jobs have been created, marking their highest levels since June 2008.
- With an unemployment rate of 3.7 percent, this is the lowest level since December, 1969 (re: rate of 10 percent/Oct, 2009 and 5.6 percent/2014).
- Only under President Trump have more than 50 percent of Americans believed it is a good time to find a quality job since Gallup began asking the question seventeen years ago.

- American families received $3.2 trillion in gross tax cuts.
- African-American, Hispanic-American, and Asian-American unemployment rates are at the lowest rates ever recorded.
- Women's unemployment rate is at the lowest rate in sixty-five years.
- Almost 3.9 million Americans have been lifted off food stamps since electing him president.
- He lowered the corporate tax rate from 35 to 21 percent so American businesses could be more competitive.
- Consumer confidence and optimism among manufacturers and small business are at all-time highs.

Now let's take a look at some of the more critical decisions this president has made since being in office—tough decisions made under tough circumstances. You really don't want to cross this president's red line or second-guess him. In just 20 months in office, he has 289 accomplishments, a list of achievements that surpasses those of President Reagan by this same point in his term, as a comparison.[7]

- **January 27, 2017:** President Trump launched a travel ban, banning visitors to travel to/from Iran, Iraq, Libya, Somalia, Sudan, Syria, and Yemen. He took heat as the media referred to it as a Muslim ban.
- **March, 2017 to present:** President Trump has initialized well over fifteen hundred deregulations on businesses to date.

7   Paul Bedard, *Washington Examiner*, Oct. 12, 2018.

- **April 7, 2017:** The United States launched fifty-nine Tomahawk cruise missiles at the Shayrat Airbase, a Syrian airfield, in retaliation for the Khan Shaykhun chemical attack, which occurred on April 4.
- **April 13, 2017:** The "Mother of all Bombs" (MOAB) was dropped for the first time in combat in an airstrike against the Islamic State of Iraq and the Levant-Khorasan Province (ISIL) tunnel complex in the Achin District in Afghanistan. This airstrike, referred to as the Nangarhar airstrike, killed ninety-four ISIS-Khorasan militants, including four commanders.
- **June 1, 2017:** President Trump withdrew the United States from the Paris Agreement on climate change that was executed on December 12, 2015.
- **October 17, 2017:** The United States declared defeat of the Islamic State.
- **November 13, 2017:** Three US aircraft carrier groups were deployed, "taking up a strike posture" near the North Korean peninsula.[8] This was the first time since 2007 that three carrier groups have worked together in the Western Pacific.
- **February 7, 2018:** President Trump proposed and the Senate passed the largest military spending bill in history: $700 billion in 2018 and $716 billion in 2019.
- **April 13, 2018:** Along with European allies, the United States launched military strikes against Syrian research, storage, and military targets, a precise "demonstration" for North Korean dictator Kim Jong-un, in my humble opinion.

---

8   Article from *The Star*, Nov. 18, 2017.

- **May 9, 2018:** The United States brought three hostages back from North Korea.
- **May 14, 2018:** The United States opens its embassy in Jerusalem, Israel, long after past presidents have committed to do the same but not followed through.
- **May 24, 2018:** President Trump pulled out of planned Summit Meeting with North Korean dictator Kim Jong-un, citing "tremendous anger and open hostility displayed in your most recent statement."
- **May 31, 2018:** President Trump imposed a 25 percent tariff on imported steel and a 10 percent tariff on imported aluminum from the European Union, Canada, and Mexico.
- **June 12, 2018:** Kim Jong-un sent leaders to meet with Secretary of State Mike Pompeo as a precursor to getting the Summit meeting in Singapore back on track. So, after sixty-five years of war on the peninsula, only time will tell if this historic face-to-face meeting will benefit the human race by the promised total denuclearization of the peninsula.
- **June 15, 2018:** President Trump hits China with $50 billion in tariffs on Chinese goods that contain industrially significant technologies.
- **July 9, 2018:** President Trump nominated Brett Kavanaugh to the Supreme Court. He was confirmed and sworn in as an associate justice on October 6, 2018.
- **July 27, 2018:** Dating back to the Korean War that was fought between June 25, 1950, and July 27, 1953, fifty-five boxes of American soldier remains were returned to the United States.

- **August 7, 2018:** Trump reimposed certain sanctions with respect to Iran.
- **August 15, 2018:** President Trump signs a proclamation adjusting steel imports into the United States, adding additional duties and tariffs.
- **September 30, 2018:** President Trump made good on his campaign pledge to renegotiate the twenty-five-year-old NAFTA deal. He negotiated a new deal with the United States-Mexico-Canada Agreement (USMCA). The new deal allows for more car and truck parts to be manufactured in North America. To have zero tariffs, 75 percent of their components must be manufactured in the USA, Canada, or Mexico. There is greater access to Canada by US dairy farmers and a sixteen-dollar wage guarantee to autoworkers.
- **October 8, 2018:** President Trump sends a US envoy to Kabul, Afghanistan, to pursue peace talks with the Taliban as they have ramped up attacks. This is America's longest war, at seventeen years thus far.

I'm curious about your thoughts on this passionate American leader who simply wants us to be the best at everything. Whether manufacturing, trade, defense, or the economy, he wants us to have it all. I believe this president truly puts Americans first and makes the tough decisions necessary to accomplish his goals. President Trump desires to be one of the greatest American presidents of all time. I certainly won't deny him that. He wants us to sleep safe at night and enjoy the fruits of our labor. We will all live better lives today and in the future because "My (Our) President Has Balls!"

ABOUT THE AUTHOR

Frank Joseph Mascetti Jr. was born in Baltimore, Maryland. After receiving his BS in electrical engineering in 1980 from the University of Maryland, College Park, he worked at Westinghouse near the Baltimore Washington International airport. He relocated to South Florida in 1981 and has been a proud resident of Boca Raton, Florida, since 1984.  For twenty-five years, he has had his own business, which represents electronics assembly and inspection equipment. Frank's strongest passions include his children, his business, his community, and, as you can tell by now, his country.

CPSIA information can be obtained
at www.ICGtesting.com
Printed in the USA
BVHW031506271219
567958BV00001B/309/P

9 781642 794342